Black Narratives of Slavery: A Very Short Introduction

VERY SHORT INTRODUCTIONS are for anyone wanting a stimulating and accessible way into a new subject. They are written by experts, and have been translated into more than 45 different languages.

The series began in 1995, and now covers a wide variety of topics in every discipline. The VSI library currently contains over 750 volumes—a Very Short Introduction to everything from Psychology and Philosophy of Science to American History and Relativity—and continues to grow in every subject area.

Very Short Introductions available now:

ABOLITIONISM Richard S. Newman
THE ABRAHAMIC RELIGIONS Charles L. Cohen
ACCOUNTING Christopher Nobes
ADDICTION Keith Humphreys
ADMINISTRATIVE LAW Stephen Thomson
ADOLESCENCE Peter K. Smith
THEODOR W. ADORNO Andrew Bowie
ADVERTISING Winston Fletcher
AERIAL WARFARE Frank Ledwidge
AESTHETICS Bence Nanay
AFRICAN AMERICAN HISTORY Jonathan Scott Holloway
AFRICAN AMERICAN RELIGION Eddie S. Glaude Jr.
AFRICAN HISTORY John Parker and Richard Rathbone
AFRICAN POLITICS Ian Taylor
AFRICAN RELIGIONS Jacob K. Olupona
AGATHA CHRISTIE Gill Plain
AGEING Nancy A. Pachana
AGNOSTICISM Robin Le Poidevin
AGRICULTURE Paul Brassley and Richard Soffe
ALEXANDER THE GREAT Hugh Bowden
ALGEBRA Peter M. Higgins
AMERICAN BUSINESS HISTORY Walter A. Friedman
AMERICAN CULTURAL HISTORY Eric Avila
AMERICAN FOREIGN RELATIONS Andrew Preston
AMERICAN HISTORY Paul S. Boyer
AMERICAN IMMIGRATION David A. Gerber
AMERICAN INTELLECTUAL HISTORY Jennifer Ratner-Rosenhagen
THE AMERICAN JUDICIAL SYSTEM Charles L. Zelden
AMERICAN LEGAL HISTORY G. Edward White
AMERICAN MILITARY HISTORY Joseph T. Glatthaar
AMERICAN NAVAL HISTORY Craig L. Symonds
AMERICAN POETRY David Caplan
AMERICAN POLITICAL HISTORY Donald Critchlow
AMERICAN POLITICAL PARTIES AND ELECTIONS L. Sandy Maisel
AMERICAN POLITICS Richard M. Valelly
THE AMERICAN PRESIDENCY Charles O. Jones
THE AMERICAN REVOLUTION Robert J. Allison
AMERICAN SLAVERY Heather Andrea Williams
THE AMERICAN SOUTH Charles Reagan Wilson
THE AMERICAN WEST Stephen Aron
AMERICAN WOMEN'S HISTORY Susan Ware
AMPHIBIANS T. S. Kemp

ANAESTHESIA Aidan O'Donnell
ANALYTIC PHILOSOPHY Michael Beaney
ANARCHISM Alex Prichard
ANCIENT ASSYRIA Karen Radner
ANCIENT EGYPT Ian Shaw
ANCIENT EGYPTIAN ART AND ARCHITECTURE Christina Riggs
ANCIENT GREECE Paul Cartledge
ANCIENT GREEK AND ROMAN SCIENCE Liba Taub
THE ANCIENT NEAR EAST Amanda H. Podany
ANCIENT PHILOSOPHY Julia Annas
ANCIENT WARFARE Harry Sidebottom
ANGELS David Albert Jones
ANGLICANISM Mark Chapman
THE ANGLO-SAXON AGE John Blair
ANIMAL BEHAVIOUR Tristram D. Wyatt
THE ANIMAL KINGDOM Peter Holland
ANIMAL RIGHTS David DeGrazia
ANSELM Thomas Williams
THE ANTARCTIC Klaus Dodds
ANTHROPOCENE Erle C. Ellis
ANTISEMITISM Steven Beller
ANXIETY Daniel Freeman and Jason Freeman
THE APOCRYPHAL GOSPELS Paul Foster
APPLIED MATHEMATICS Alain Goriely
THOMAS AQUINAS Fergus Kerr
ARBITRATION Thomas Schultz and Thomas Grant
ARCHAEOLOGY Paul Bahn
ARCHITECTURE Andrew Ballantyne
THE ARCTIC Klaus Dodds and Jamie Woodward
HANNAH ARENDT Dana Villa
ARISTOCRACY William Doyle
ARISTOTLE Jonathan Barnes
ART HISTORY Dana Arnold
ART THEORY Cynthia Freeland
ARTIFICIAL INTELLIGENCE Margaret A. Boden
ASIAN AMERICAN HISTORY Madeline Y. Hsu
ASTROBIOLOGY David C. Catling
ASTROPHYSICS James Binney
ATHEISM Julian Baggini
THE ATMOSPHERE Paul I. Palmer
AUGUSTINE Henry Chadwick
JANE AUSTEN Tom Keymer
AUSTRALIA Kenneth Morgan
AUTHORITARIANISM James Loxton
AUTISM Uta Frith
AUTOBIOGRAPHY Laura Marcus
THE AVANT GARDE David Cottington
THE AZTECS Davíd Carrasco
BABYLONIA Trevor Bryce
BACTERIA Sebastian G. B. Amyes
BANKING John Goddard and John O. S. Wilson
BARTHES Jonathan Culler
THE BEATS David Sterritt
BEAUTY Roger Scruton
LUDWIG VAN BEETHOVEN Mark Evan Bonds
BEHAVIOURAL ECONOMICS Michelle Baddeley
BESTSELLERS John Sutherland
THE BIBLE John Riches
BIBLICAL ARCHAEOLOGY Eric H. Cline
BIG DATA Dawn E. Holmes
BIOCHEMISTRY Mark Lorch
BIODIVERSITY CONSERVATION David Macdonald
BIOGEOGRAPHY Mark V. Lomolino
BIOGRAPHY Hermione Lee
BIOMETRICS Michael Fairhurst
ELIZABETH BISHOP Jonathan F. S. Post
BLACK HOLES Katherine Blundell
BLACK NARRATIVES OF SLAVERY Robert J. Patterson
BLASPHEMY Yvonne Sherwood
BLOOD Chris Cooper
THE BLUES Elijah Wald
THE BODY Chris Shilling
THE BOHEMIANS David Weir
NIELS BOHR J. L. Heilbron
THE BOOK OF COMMON PRAYER Brian Cummings
THE BOOK OF MORMON Terryl Givens

BORDERS Alexander C. Diener and Joshua Hagen
JORGE LUIS BORGES Ilan Stavans
THE BRAIN Michael O'Shea
BRANDING Robert Jones
THE BRICS Andrew F. Cooper
BRITISH ARCHITECTURE Dana Arnold
BRITISH CINEMA Charles Barr
THE BRITISH CONSTITUTION Martin Loughlin
THE BRITISH EMPIRE Ashley Jackson
BRITISH POLITICS Tony Wright
BUDDHA Michael Carrithers
BUDDHISM Damien Keown
BUDDHIST ETHICS Damien Keown
BYZANTIUM Peter Sarris
CALVINISM Jon Balserak
ALBERT CAMUS Oliver Gloag
CANADA Donald Wright
CANCER Nicholas James
CAPITALISM James Fulcher
CATHOLICISM Gerald O'Collins
THE CATHOLIC REFORMATION James E. Kelly
CAUSATION Stephen Mumford and Rani Lill Anjum
THE CELL Terence Allen and Graham Cowling
THE CELTS Barry Cunliffe
CHAOS Leonard Smith
GEOFFREY CHAUCER David Wallace
CHEMISTRY Peter Atkins
CHILD PSYCHOLOGY Usha Goswami
CHILDREN'S LITERATURE Kimberley Reynolds
CHINESE LITERATURE Sabina Knight
CHOICE THEORY Michael Allingham
CHRISTIAN ART Beth Williamson
CHRISTIAN ETHICS D. Stephen Long
CHRISTIANITY Linda Woodhead
CICERO Yelena Baraz
CIRCADIAN RHYTHMS Russell Foster and Leon Kreitzman
CITIZENSHIP Richard Bellamy
CITY PLANNING Carl Abbott
CIVIL ENGINEERING David Muir Wood
THE CIVIL RIGHTS MOVEMENT Thomas C. Holt
CIVIL WARS Monica Duffy Toft
CLASSICAL LITERATURE William Allan
CLASSICAL MYTHOLOGY Helen Morales
CLASSICS Mary Beard and John Henderson
CLAUSEWITZ Michael Howard
CLIMATE Mark Maslin
CLIMATE CHANGE Mark Maslin
CLINICAL PSYCHOLOGY Susan Llewelyn and Katie Aafjes-van Doorn
COGNITIVE BEHAVIOURAL THERAPY Freda McManus
COGNITIVE NEUROSCIENCE Richard Passingham
THE COLD WAR Robert J. McMahon
COLONIAL AMERICA Alan Taylor
COLONIAL LATIN AMERICAN LITERATURE Rolena Adorno
COMBINATORICS Robin Wilson
COMEDY Matthew Bevis
COMMUNISM Leslie Holmes
COMPARATIVE LAW Sabrina Ragone and Guido Smorto
COMPARATIVE LITERATURE Ben Hutchinson
COMPETITION AND ANTITRUST LAW Ariel Ezrachi
COMPLEXITY John H. Holland
THE COMPUTER Darrel Ince
COMPUTER SCIENCE Subrata Dasgupta
CONCENTRATION CAMPS Dan Stone
CONDENSED MATTER PHYSICS Ross H. McKenzie
CONFUCIANISM Daniel K. Gardner
THE CONQUISTADORS Matthew Restall and Felipe Fernández-Armesto
CONSCIENCE Paul Strohm
CONSCIOUSNESS Susan Blackmore
CONTEMPORARY ART Julian Stallabrass
CONTEMPORARY FICTION Robert Eaglestone
CONTINENTAL PHILOSOPHY Simon Critchley
COPERNICUS Owen Gingerich
CORAL REEFS Charles Sheppard

CORPORATE SOCIAL RESPONSIBILITY Jeremy Moon
CORRUPTION Leslie Holmes
COSMOLOGY Peter Coles
COUNTRY MUSIC Richard Carlin
CREATIVITY Vlad Glăveanu
CRIME FICTION Richard Bradford
CRIMINAL JUSTICE Julian V. Roberts
CRIMINOLOGY Tim Newburn
CRITICAL THEORY Stephen Eric Bronner
THE CRUSADES Christopher Tyerman
CRYPTOGRAPHY Sean Murphy and Rachel Player
CRYSTALLOGRAPHY A. M. Glazer
THE CULTURAL REVOLUTION Richard Curt Kraus
DADA AND SURREALISM David Hopkins
DANTE Peter Hainsworth and David Robey
DARWIN Jonathan Howard
THE DEAD SEA SCROLLS Timothy H. Lim
DECADENCE David Weir
DECOLONIZATION Dane Kennedy
DEMENTIA Kathleen Taylor
DEMOCRACY Naomi Zack
DEMOGRAPHY Sarah Harper
DEPRESSION Jan Scott and Mary Jane Tacchi
DERRIDA Simon Glendinning
DESCARTES Tom Sorell
DESERTS Nick Middleton
DESIGN John Heskett
DEVELOPMENT Ian Goldin
DEVELOPMENTAL BIOLOGY Lewis Wolpert
THE DEVIL Darren Oldridge
DIASPORA Kevin Kenny
CHARLES DICKENS Jenny Hartley
DICTIONARIES Lynda Mugglestone
DINOSAURS David Norman
DIPLOMATIC HISTORY Joseph M. Siracusa
DOCUMENTARY FILM Patricia Aufderheide
DOSTOEVSKY Deborah Martinsen
DREAMING J. Allan Hobson
DRUGS Les Iversen
DRUIDS Barry Cunliffe
DYNASTY Jeroen Duindam
DYSLEXIA Margaret J. Snowling
EARLY MUSIC Thomas Forrest Kelly
THE EARTH Martin Redfern
EARTH SYSTEM SCIENCE Tim Lenton
ECOLOGY Jaboury Ghazoul
ECONOMICS Partha Dasgupta
EDUCATION Gary Thomas
EGYPTIAN MYTH Geraldine Pinch
EIGHTEENTH-CENTURY BRITAIN Paul Langford
ELECTIONS L. Sandy Maisel and Jennifer A. Yoder
THE ELEMENTS Philip Ball
GEORGE ELIOT Juliette Atkinson
EMOTION Dylan Evans
EMPIRE Stephen Howe
EMPLOYMENT LAW David Cabrelli
ENERGY SYSTEMS Nick Jenkins
ENGELS Terrell Carver
ENGINEERING David Blockley
THE ENGLISH LANGUAGE Simon Horobin
ENGLISH LITERATURE Jonathan Bate
THE ENLIGHTENMENT John Robertson
ENTREPRENEURSHIP Paul Westhead and Mike Wright
ENTROPY James Binney
ENVIRONMENTAL ECONOMICS Stephen Smith
ENVIRONMENTAL ETHICS Robin Attfield
ENVIRONMENTAL JUSTICE Pamela Hill
ENVIRONMENTAL LAW Elizabeth Fisher
ENVIRONMENTAL POLITICS Andrew Dobson
ENZYMES Paul Engel
THE EPIC Anthony Welch
EPICUREANISM Catherine Wilson
EPIDEMIOLOGY Rodolfo Saracci
ETHICS Simon Blackburn
ETHNOMUSICOLOGY Timothy Rice
THE ETRUSCANS Christopher Smith
EUGENICS Philippa Levine
THE EUROPEAN UNION Simon Usherwood and John Pinder

EUROPEAN UNION LAW
Anthony Arnull
EVANGELICALISM
John G. Stackhouse Jr.
EVIL Luke Russell
EVOLUTION Brian and Deborah Charlesworth
EXISTENTIALISM Thomas Flynn
EXPLORATION Stewart A. Weaver
EXTINCTION Paul B. Wignall
THE EYE Michael Land
FAIRY TALE Marina Warner
FAITH Roger Trigg
FAMILY LAW Jonathan Herring
MICHAEL FARADAY
Frank A. J. L. James
FASCISM Kevin Passmore
FASHION Rebecca Arnold
FEDERALISM Mark J. Rozell and Clyde Wilcox
FEMINISM Margaret Walters
FEMINIST PHILOSOPHY
Katharine Jenkins
FILM Michael Wood
FILM MUSIC Kathryn Kalinak
FILM NOIR James Naremore
FIRE Andrew C. Scott
THE FIRST WORLD WAR
Michael Howard
FLUID MECHANICS Eric Lauga
FOLK MUSIC Mark Slobin
FOOD John Krebs
FORENSIC PSYCHOLOGY
David Canter
FORENSIC SCIENCE Jim Fraser
FORESTS Jaboury Ghazoul
FOSSILS Keith Thomson
FOUCAULT Gary Gutting
THE FOUNDING FATHERS
R. B. Bernstein
FRACTALS Kenneth Falconer
FREE SPEECH Nigel Warburton
FREE WILL Thomas Pink
FREEMASONRY Andreas Önnerfors
FRENCH CINEMA Dudley Andrew
FRENCH LITERATURE John D. Lyons
FRENCH PHILOSOPHY
Stephen Gaukroger and Knox Peden
THE FRENCH REVOLUTION
William Doyle
FREUD Anthony Storr
FUNDAMENTALISM Malise Ruthven
FUNGI Nicholas P. Money
THE FUTURE Jennifer M. Gidley
FUTURSM Ara Merjian
GALAXIES John Gribbin
GALILEO Stillman Drake
GAME THEORY Ken Binmore
GANDHI Bhikhu Parekh
GARDEN HISTORY Gordon Campbell
GENDER HISTORY Antoinette Burton
GENES Jonathan Slack
GENIUS Andrew Robinson
GENOMICS John Archibald
GEOGRAPHY John Matthews and David Herbert
GEOLOGY Jan Zalasiewicz
GEOMETRY Maciej Dunajski
GEOPHYSICAL AND CLIMATE HAZARDS Bill McGuire
GEOPHYSICS William Lowrie
GEOPOLITICS Klaus Dodds
GERMAN LITERATURE Nicholas Boyle
GERMAN PHILOSOPHY
Andrew Bowie
THE GHETTO Bryan Cheyette
GLACIATION David J. A. Evans
GLOBAL ECONOMIC HISTORY
Robert C. Allen
GLOBAL ISLAM Nile Green
GLOBALIZATION Manfred B. Steger
GOD John Bowker
GÖDEL'S THEOREM A. W. Moore
GOETHE Ritchie Robertson
THE GOTHIC Nick Groom
GOVERNANCE Mark Bevir
GRAVITY Timothy Clifton
THE GREAT DEPRESSION AND THE NEW DEAL Eric Rauchway
THE GULAG Alan Barenberg
HABEAS CORPUS Amanda L. Tyler
HABERMAS James Gordon Finlayson
THE HABSBURG EMPIRE
Martyn Rady
HAPPINESS Daniel M. Haybron
THE HARLEM RENAISSANCE
Cheryl A. Wall
THE HEBREW BIBLE AS LITERATURE Tod Linafelt
HEGEL Peter Singer

HEIDEGGER Michael Inwood
THE HELLENISTIC AGE Peter Thonemann
HEREDITY John Waller
HERMENEUTICS Jens Zimmermann
HERODOTUS Jennifer T. Roberts
HIEROGLYPHS Penelope Wilson
HINDUISM Kim Knott
HISTORY John H. Arnold
THE HISTORY OF ASTRONOMY Michael Hoskin
THE HISTORY OF CHEMISTRY William H. Brock
THE HISTORY OF CHILDHOOD James Marten
THE HISTORY OF CINEMA Geoffrey Nowell-Smith
THE HISTORY OF COMPUTING Doron Swade
THE HISTORY OF EMOTIONS Thomas Dixon
THE HISTORY OF LIFE Michael Benton
THE HISTORY OF MATHEMATICS Jacqueline Stedall
THE HISTORY OF MEDICINE William Bynum
THE HISTORY OF PHYSICS J. L. Heilbron
THE HISTORY OF POLITICAL THOUGHT Richard Whatmore
THE HISTORY OF TIME Leofranc Holford-Strevens
HIV AND AIDS Alan Whiteside
HOBBES Richard Tuck
HOLLYWOOD Peter Decherney
THE HOLY ROMAN EMPIRE Joachim Whaley
HOME Michael Allen Fox
HOMER Barbara Graziosi
HORACE Llewelyn Morgan
HORMONES Martin Luck
HORROR Darryl Jones
HUMAN ANATOMY Leslie Klenerman
HUMAN EVOLUTION Bernard Wood
HUMAN GEOGRAPHY Patricia Daley and Ian Klinke
HUMANITARIANISM Julia F. Irwin
HUMAN PHYSIOLOGY Jamie A. Davies
HUMAN RESOURCE MANAGEMENT Adrian Wilkinson
HUMAN RIGHTS Andrew Clapham
HUMANISM Stephen Law
HUME James A. Harris
HUMOUR Noël Carroll
IBN SĪNĀ (AVICENNA) Peter Adamson
THE ICE AGE Jamie Woodward
IDENTITY Florian Coulmas
IDEOLOGY Michael Freeden
IMAGINATION Jennifer Gosetti-Ferencei
THE IMMUNE SYSTEM Paul Klenerman
INDIAN CINEMA Ashish Rajadhyaksha
INDIAN PHILOSOPHY Sue Hamilton
THE INDUSTRIAL REVOLUTION Robert C. Allen
INFECTIOUS DISEASE Marta L. Wayne and Benjamin M. Bolker
INFINITY Ian Stewart
INFORMATION Luciano Floridi
INNOVATION Mark Dodgson and David Gann
INTELLECTUAL PROPERTY Siva Vaidhyanathan
INTELLIGENCE Ian J. Deary
INTERNATIONAL LAW Vaughan Lowe
INTERNATIONAL MIGRATION Khalid Koser
INTERNATIONAL RELATIONS Christian Reus-Smit
INTERNATIONAL SECURITY Christopher S. Browning
INSECTS Simon Leather
INVASIVE SPECIES Julie Lockwood and Dustin Welbourne
IRAN Ali M. Ansari
THE IRAQ WARS Samuel Helfont
ISLAM Malise Ruthven
ISLAMIC HISTORY Adam Silverstein
ISLAMIC LAW Mashood A. Baderin
ISOTOPES Rob Ellam
ITALIAN LITERATURE Peter Hainsworth and David Robey
HENRY JAMES Susan L. Mizruchi
JAPANESE LITERATURE Alan Tansman

JESUS Richard Bauckham
JEWISH HISTORY David N. Myers
JEWISH LITERATURE Ilan Stavans
JOURNALISM Ian Hargreaves
JAMES JOYCE Colin MacCabe
JUDAISM Norman Solomon
JUNG Anthony Stevens
THE JURY Renée Lettow Lerner
KABBALAH Joseph Dan
KAFKA Ritchie Robertson
KANT Roger Scruton
KEYNES Robert Skidelsky
KIERKEGAARD Patrick Gardiner
KNOWLEDGE Jennifer Nagel
THE KORAN Michael Cook
KOREA Michael J. Seth
LAKES Warwick F. Vincent
LANDSCAPE ARCHITECTURE
Ian H. Thompson
LANDSCAPES AND
GEOMORPHOLOGY
Andrew Goudie and Heather Viles
LANGUAGES Stephen R. Anderson
LATE ANTIQUITY Gillian Clark
LAW Raymond Wacks
THE LAWS OF THERMODYNAMICS
Peter Atkins
LEADERSHIP Keith Grint
LEARNING Mark Haselgrove
LEIBNIZ Maria Rosa Antognazza
C. S. LEWIS James Como
LIBERALISM Michael Freeden
LIGHT Ian Walmsley
LINCOLN Allen C. Guelzo
LINGUISTICS Peter Matthews
LITERARY THEORY Jonathan Culler
LOCKE John Dunn
LOGIC Graham Priest
LOVE Ronald de Sousa
MARTIN LUTHER Scott H. Hendrix
MACHIAVELLI Quentin Skinner
MADNESS Andrew Scull
MAGIC Owen Davies
MAGNA CARTA Nicholas Vincent
MAGNETISM Stephen Blundell
MOSES MAIMONIDES Ross Brann
MALTHUS Donald Winch
MAMMALS T. S. Kemp
MANAGEMENT John Hendry
NELSON MANDELA Elleke Boehmer
MAO Delia Davin
MARINE BIOLOGY Philip V. Mladenov
MARKETING
Kenneth Le Meunier-FitzHugh
THE MARQUIS DE SADE John Phillips
MARTYRDOM Jolyon Mitchell
MARX Peter Singer
MATERIALS Christopher Hall
MATHEMATICAL ANALYSIS
Richard Earl
MATHEMATICAL BIOLOGY
Philip K. Maini
MATHEMATICAL FINANCE
Mark H. A. Davis
MATHEMATICS Timothy Gowers
MATTER Geoff Cottrell
THE MAYA Matthew Restall and
Amara Solari
MEANING Emma Borg and
Sarah A. Fisher
THE MEANING OF LIFE Terry Eagleton
MEASUREMENT David Hand
MEDICAL ETHICS Michael Dunn and
Tony Hope
MEDICAL LAW Charles Foster
MEDIEVAL BRITAIN John Gillingham
and Ralph A. Griffiths
MEDIEVAL LITERATURE
Elaine Treharne
MEDIEVAL PHILOSOPHY
John Marenbon
HERMAN MELVILLE Maurice S. Lee
MEMORY Jonathan K. Foster
METAPHYSICS Stephen Mumford
METHODISM William J. Abraham
THE MEXICAN REVOLUTION
Alan Knight
MICROBIOLOGY Nicholas P. Money
MICROBIOMES Angela E. Douglas
MICROECONOMICS Avinash Dixit
MICROSCOPY Terence Allen
THE MIDDLE AGES Miri Rubin
MILITARY JUSTICE Eugene R. Fidell
MILITARY STRATEGY
Antulio J. Echevarria II
JOHN STUART MILL Gregory Claeys
MINERALS David Vaughan
MIRACLES Yujin Nagasawa
MODERN ARCHITECTURE Adam Sharr
MODERN ART David Cottington

MODERN BRAZIL Anthony W. Pereira
MODERN CHINA Rana Mitter
MODERN DRAMA Kirsten E. Shepherd-Barr
MODERN FRANCE Vanessa R. Schwartz
MODERN INDIA Craig Jeffrey
MODERN IRELAND Senia Pašeta
MODERN ITALY Anna Cento Bull
MODERN JAPAN Christopher Goto-Jones
MODERN LATIN AMERICAN LITERATURE Roberto González Echevarría
MODERN WAR Richard English
MODERNISM Christopher Butler
MOLECULAR BIOLOGY Aysha Divan and Janice A. Royds
MOLECULES Philip Ball
MONASTICISM Stephen J. Davis
THE MONGOLS Morris Rossabi
MONTAIGNE William M. Hamlin
MOONS David A. Rothery
THOMAS MORE Peter Marshall
MORMONISM Richard Lyman Bushman
MOUNTAINS Martin F. Price
MUHAMMAD Jonathan A. C. Brown
MULTICULTURALISM Ali Rattansi
MULTILINGUALISM John C. Maher
MUSIC Nicholas Cook
MUSIC AND TECHNOLOGY Mark Katz
MYTH Robert A. Segal
NANOTECHNOLOGY Philip Moriarty
NAPOLEON David A. Bell
THE NAPOLEONIC WARS Mike Rapport
NATIONALISM Steven Grosby
NATIVE AMERICAN LITERATURE Sean Teuton
NAVIGATION Jim Bennett
NAZI GERMANY Jane Caplan
NEGOTIATION Carrie Menkel-Meadow
NEOLIBERALISM Manfred B. Steger and Ravi K. Roy
NETWORKS Guido Caldarelli and Michele Catanzaro
NEURODIVERSITY Robert Chapman and Sue Fletcher-Watson
THE NEW TESTAMENT Luke Timothy Johnson
THE NEW TESTAMENT AS LITERATURE Kyle Keefer
NEWTON Robert Iliffe
NIETZSCHE Michael Tanner
NINETEENTH-CENTURY BRITAIN Christopher Harvie and H. C. G. Matthew
THE NORMAN CONQUEST George Garnett
NORTH AMERICAN INDIANS Theda Perdue and Michael D. Green
NORTHERN IRELAND Marc Mulholland
NOTHING Frank Close
NUCLEAR PHYSICS Frank Close
NUCLEAR POWER Maxwell Irvine
NUCLEAR WEAPONS Joseph M. Siracusa
NUMBER THEORY Robin Wilson
NUMBERS Peter M. Higgins
NUTRITION David A. Bender
OBJECTIVITY Stephen Gaukroger
OBSERVATIONAL ASTRONOMY Geoff Cottrell
OCEANS Dorrik Stow
THE OLD TESTAMENT Michael D. Coogan
ORAL HISTORY Douglas A. Boyd
THE ORCHESTRA D. Kern Holoman
ORGANIC CHEMISTRY Graham Patrick
ORGANIZATIONS Mary Jo Hatch
ORGANIZED CRIME Georgios A. Antonopoulos and Georgios Papanicolaou
ORTHODOX CHRISTIANITY A. Edward Siecienski
OVID Llewelyn Morgan
PAGANISM Owen Davies
PAKISTAN Pippa Virdee
THE PALESTINIAN-ISRAELI CONFLICT Martin Bunton
PANDEMICS Christian W. McMillen
PARTICLE PHYSICS Frank Close
PAUL E. P. Sanders
IVAN PAVLOV Daniel P. Todes
PEACE Oliver P. Richmond
PENTECOSTALISM William K. Kay

PERCEPTION Brian Rogers
THE PERIODIC TABLE Eric R. Scerri
PHILOSOPHICAL METHOD
Timothy Williamson
PHILOSOPHY Edward Craig
PHILOSOPHY IN THE ISLAMIC WORLD Peter Adamson
PHILOSOPHY OF BIOLOGY
Samir Okasha
PHILOSOPHY OF LAW
Raymond Wacks
PHILOSOPHY OF MIND
Barbara Gail Montero
PHILOSOPHY OF PHYSICS
David Wallace
PHILOSOPHY OF SCIENCE
Samir Okasha
PHILOSOPHY OF RELIGION
Tim Bayne
PHOTOGRAPHY Steve Edwards
PHYSICAL CHEMISTRY Peter Atkins
PHYSICS Sidney Perkowitz
PILGRIMAGE Ian Reader
PLAGUE Paul Slack
PLANETARY SYSTEMS
Raymond T. Pierrehumbert
PLANETS David A. Rothery
PLANTS Timothy Walker
PLATE TECTONICS Peter Molnar
SYLVIA PLATH Heather Clark
PLATO Julia Annas
POETRY Bernard O'Donoghue
POLITICAL PHILOSOPHY David Miller
POLITICS Kenneth Minogue
POLYGAMY Sarah M. S. Pearsall
POPULISM Cas Mudde and Cristóbal Rovira Kaltwasser
POSTCOLONIALISM
Robert J. C. Young
POSTMODERNISM Christopher Butler
POSTSTRUCTURALISM
Catherine Belsey
POSTWAR EUROPE Richard Bessel
POVERTY Philip N. Jefferson
PREHISTORY Chris Gosden
PRESOCRATIC PHILOSOPHY
Catherine Osborne
PRIVACY Raymond Wacks
PROBABILITY John Haigh
PROGRESSIVISM Walter Nugent
PROHIBITION W. J. Rorabaugh
PROJECTS Andrew Davies
PROTESTANTISM Mark A. Noll
MARCEL PROUST Joshua Landy
PSEUDOSCIENCE Michael D. Gordin
PSYCHIATRY Tom Burns
PSYCHOANALYSIS Daniel Pick
PSYCHOLINGUISTICS
Ferenda Ferreria
PSYCHOLOGY Gillian Butler and Freda McManus
PSYCHOLOGY OF MUSIC
Elizabeth Hellmuth Margulis
PSYCHOPATHY Essi Viding
PSYCHOTHERAPY Tom Burns and Eva Burns-Lundgren
PUBLIC ADMINISTRATION
Stella Z. Theodoulou and Ravi K. Roy
PUBLIC HEALTH Virginia Berridge
PURITANISM Francis J. Bremer
THE QUAKERS Pink Dandelion
QUANTUM THEORY
John Polkinghorne
RACISM Ali Rattansi
RADIOACTIVITY Claudio Tuniz
RASTAFARI Ennis B. Edmonds
READING Belinda Jack
THE REAGAN REVOLUTION Gil Troy
REALITY Jan Westerhoff
RECONSTRUCTION Allen C. Guelzo
THE REFORMATION Peter Marshall
REFUGEES Gil Loescher
RELATIVITY Russell Stannard
RELIGION Thomas A. Tweed
RELIGION IN AMERICA
Timothy Beal
THE RENAISSANCE Jerry Brotton
RENAISSANCE ART
Geraldine A. Johnson
RENEWABLE ENERGY Nick Jelley
REPTILES T. S. Kemp
REVOLUTIONS Jack A. Goldstone
RHETORIC Richard Toye
RISK Baruch Fischhoff and John Kadvany
RITUAL Barry Stephenson
RIVERS Nick Middleton
ROBOTICS Alan Winfield
ROCK "N" ROLL Elijah Wald
ROCKS Jan Zalasiewicz

ROMAN BRITAIN Peter Salway
THE ROMAN EMPIRE Christopher Kelly
THE ROMAN REPUBLIC David M. Gwynn
ROMANTICISM Michael Ferber
ROUSSEAU Robert Wokler
THE RULE OF LAW Aziz Z. Huq
RUSSELL A. C. Grayling
THE RUSSIAN ECONOMY Richard Connolly
RUSSIAN HISTORY Geoffrey Hosking
RUSSIAN LITERATURE Catriona Kelly
RUSSIAN POLITICS Brian D. Taylor
THE RUSSIAN REVOLUTION S. A. Smith
SAINTS Simon Yarrow
SAMURAI Michael Wert
SAVANNAS Peter A. Furley
SCEPTICISM Duncan Pritchard
SCHIZOPHRENIA Chris Frith and Eve Johnstone
SCHOPENHAUER Christopher Janaway
SCIENCE AND RELIGION Thomas Dixon and Adam R. Shapiro
SCIENCE FICTION David Seed
THE SCIENTIFIC REVOLUTION Lawrence M. Principe
SCOTLAND Rab Houston
SECULARISM Andrew Copson
THE SELF Marya Schechtman
SEXUAL SELECTION Marlene Zuk and Leigh W. Simmons
SEXUALITY Véronique Mottier
WILLIAM SHAKESPEARE Stanley Wells
SHAKESPEARE'S COMEDIES Bart van Es
SHAKESPEARE'S SONNETS AND POEMS Jonathan F. S. Post
SHAKESPEARE'S TRAGEDIES Stanley Wells
GEORGE BERNARD SHAW Christopher Wixson
MARY SHELLEY Charlotte Gordon
THE SHORT STORY Andrew Kahn
SIKHISM Eleanor Nesbitt
SILENT FILM Donna Kornhaber
THE SILK ROAD James A. Millward
SLANG Jonathon Green
SLEEP Steven W. Lockley and Russell G. Foster
SMELL Matthew Cobb
ADAM SMITH Christopher J. Berry
SOCIAL AND CULTURAL ANTHROPOLOGY John Monaghan and Peter Just
SOCIALISM Michael Newman
SOCIAL PSYCHOLOGY Richard J. Crisp
SOCIAL SCIENCE Alexander Betts
SOCIAL WORK Sally Holland and Jonathan Scourfield
SOCIOLINGUISTICS John Edwards
SOCIOLOGY Steve Bruce
SOCRATES C. C. W. Taylor
SOFT MATTER Tom McLeish
SOPHOCLES Edith Hall
SOUND Mike Goldsmith
SOUTHEAST ASIA James R. Rush
THE SOVIET UNION Stephen Lovell
THE SPANISH CIVIL WAR Helen Graham
SPANISH LITERATURE Jo Labanyi
THE SPARTANS Andrew J. Bayliss
SPINOZA Roger Scruton
SPIRITUALITY Philip Sheldrake
SPORT Mike Cronin
STARS Andrew King
STATISTICS David J. Hand
STEM CELLS Jonathan Slack
STOICISM Brad Inwood
STRUCTURAL ENGINEERING David Blockley
STUART BRITAIN John Morrill
SUBURBS Carl Abbott
THE SUN Philip Judge
SUPERCONDUCTIVITY Stephen Blundell
SUPERSTITION Stuart Vyse
SURVEILLANCE David Lyon
SUSTAINABILITY Saleem Ali
SYMBIOSIS Nancy A. Moran
SYMMETRY Ian Stewart
SYNAESTHESIA Julia Simner
SYNTHETIC BIOLOGY Jamie A. Davies
SYSTEMS BIOLOGY Eberhard O. Voit
TAXATION Stephen Smith
TEETH Peter S. Ungar
TERRORISM Charles Townshend
THEATRE Marvin Carlson

THEOLOGY David F. Ford
THINKING AND REASONING Jonathan St B. T. Evans
HENRY DAVID THOREAU Lawrence Buell
THOUGHT Tim Bayne
THUCYDIDES Jennifer T. Roberts
TIBETAN BUDDHISM Matthew T. Kapstein
TIDES David George Bowers and Emyr Martyn Roberts
TIME Jenann Ismael
TOCQUEVILLE Harvey C. Mansfield
TOLERATION Andrew Murphy
J. R. R. TOLKIEN Matthew Townend
LEO TOLSTOY Liza Knapp
TOPOLOGY Richard Earl
TRAGEDY Adrian Poole
TRANSLATION Matthew Reynolds
THE TREATY OF VERSAILLES Michael S. Neiberg
TRIGONOMETRY Glen Van Brummelen
THE TROJAN WAR Eric H. Cline
ANTHONY TROLLOPE Dinah Birch
TRUST Katherine Hawley
THE TUDORS John Guy
TWENTIETH-CENTURY BRITAIN Kenneth O. Morgan
TYPOGRAPHY Paul Luna
THE UNITED NATIONS Jussi M. Hanhimäki
UNIVERSITIES AND COLLEGES David Palfreyman and Paul Temple
THE U.S. CIVIL WAR Louis P. Masur
THE U.S. CONGRESS Donald A. Ritchie
THE U.S. CONSTITUTION David J. Bodenhamer
THE U.S. SUPREME COURT Linda Greenhouse
UTILITARIANISM Katarzyna de Lazari-Radek and Peter Singer
UTOPIANISM Lyman Tower Sargent
VATICAN II Shaun Blanchard and Stephen Bullivant
VETERINARY SCIENCE James Yeates
THE VICTORIANS Martin Hewitt
THE VIKINGS Julian D. Richards
VIOLENCE Philip Dwyer
THE VIRGIN MARY Mary Joan Winn Leith
THE VIRTUES Craig A. Boyd and Kevin Timpe
VIRUSES Dorothy H. Crawford
VOLCANOES Michael J. Branney and Jan Zalasiewicz
VOLTAIRE Nicholas Cronk
WAR AND RELIGION Jolyon Mitchell and Joshua Rey
WAR AND TECHNOLOGY Alex Roland
WATER John Finney
WAVES Mike Goldsmith
WEATHER Storm Dunlop
SIMONE WEIL A. Rebecca Rozelle-Stone
THE WELFARE STATE David Garland
WITCHCRAFT Malcolm Gaskill
WITTGENSTEIN A. C. Grayling
WORK Stephen Fineman
WORLD MUSIC Philip Bohlman
WORLD MYTHOLOGY David Leeming
THE WORLD TRADE ORGANIZATION Amrita Narlikar
WORLD WAR II Gerhard L. Weinberg
WRITING AND SCRIPT Andrew Robinson
ZIONISM Michael Stanislawski
ÉMILE ZOLA Brian Nelson

Available soon:

AEROSPACE ENGINEERING John Baker
MORAL RESPONSIBILITY Paul Russell

Robert J. Patterson

BLACK NARRATIVES OF SLAVERY

A Very Short Introduction

OXFORD
UNIVERSITY PRESS

Oxford University Press is a department of the University of Oxford. It furthers the University's objective of excellence in research, scholarship, and education by publishing worldwide. Oxford is a registered trade mark of Oxford University Press in the UK and in certain other countries.

Published in the United States of America by Oxford University Press
198 Madison Avenue, New York, NY 10016, United States of America.

CIP data is on file at the Library of Congress.

ISBN 9780197678374

DOI: 10.1093/9780197678404.001.0001

Printed by Integrated Books International, United States of America

The manufacturer's authorized representative in the EU for product safety is Oxford University Press España S.A. of Parque Empresarial San Fernando de Henares, Avenida de Castilla, 2 – 28830 Madrid (www.oup.es/en or product.safety@oup.com). OUP España S.A. also acts as importer into Spain of products made by the manufacturer.

To Radical Truth, and even more,
to Radical Acceptance

Contents

List of illustrations

Acknowledgments

Even a short book incurs a debt—a debt of gratitude, that is. I am happy, in these acknowledgments, to pay up and to pay it forward.

A Georgetown University Research Leave and a Summer Salary Supplement provided me with the precious time that I needed to research, think about, and write this book. I appreciate the Provost's Office for its commitment to making generous resources available for faculty to complete their research.

Thank you to Oxford University Press Senior Acquisitions Editor Lucy Randall for shepherding the project to completion after Nancy Toff, who signed me to this project, retired, and Project Editor Imogene Haslam for ensuring the book was ready for production and publication.

Writing in community helped this project. Not only did the Writing Group provide accountability for submitting work, but it created a vibrant space to exchange ideas. Cheers to Dana Williams, Gershun Avilez, Anita Gonzalez, Corey Fields, Brienne Adams, Kristia Wantchekon, Rosemary Ndubuizu, Carla Shedd, Melanie White, Soyica Colbert, Dayo Gore, Amani Morrison, and Mecca Sullivan for their helpful insights.

L. H. Stallings read a draft of the introduction, and, as she always does, provided perceptive feedback. And, of course, Soyica D. Colbert, as she has done each other time, read the entire manuscript, in addition to serving as an ongoing interlocutor throughout the writing and revision processes. No project would come to fruition without Aida Levy-Hussen's insights as well. For their generosities, many thanks.

Life changed significantly for me between when I began writing this book and when I finished it. On June 17, 2024, my aunt, Glenda F. Patterson, concluded her battle with metastatic breast cancer, and took her final rest. The journey to the loss—and the loss itself—shifted my world and outlook in some specific and general ways. For her memory and legacy, I am grateful. Her spirit that lives anchored the completion of this book, and because He lives, I continue to face tomorrow.

I have friends, family, and loved ones who consistently supported the completion of this book in explicit and implicit ways, asking about its status, wanting to buy it when it is published, sending me food to ensure I had uninterrupted time to write, telling other (random) people about this book (and my others), and the list goes on of how they showed their love and support: Tiffany Craig, Michelle Wallace, Tiffany Donelson, Ebony Walden, Jason Simmonds, Zandria F. Robinson, Demetra Andrews, Ty Williams, O. Sherry Akande, Daniel Harris, Linda Blair, Anjulet Tucker, Susana Morris, Meghan Callier, Conitras M. Dickens, Wallrick Williams, Michael Awkward, Angelyn Mitchell, Shirley Williams, Pauline Greer, and Marcilyn Patterson.

And last, but certainly not least, I extend tremendous love and gratitude to my mother, Doris J. Patterson, not only for the gift of life, but for championing this book, encouraging its completion, and looking forward to its publication.

May Truth Prevail.

Chapter 1
Black narratives of slavery and Black cultural production

The arrival of Afro-descendant people on the shores of Jamestown, Virginia, in 1619 turned a new chapter in what would become one of the most pivotal eras in American history—the pre-Emancipation era. While the captives technically were not enslaved, they were treated as commodities and their exchange did contribute to the type of enslavement that became chattel slavery. This year in American history, while noted, often gets overshadowed by 1776, the year the United States' colonies declared their independence from Great Britain. Although the nation did not believe Great Britain should enslave it, or deny it the rights it believed it deserved, the founding fathers ignored the irony of an emerging nation that championed freedom and independence while maintaining slavery for African descendants. For many students of history, 1776 marks the year of the nation's official founding.

Nikole Hannah-Jones's *The 1619 Project*, however, compellingly has suggested that 1619 becomes an alternative, original founding year. For Jones, this founding date 157 years earlier appropriately ties the beginning of American history to the beginnings of the transatlantic slave trade in the North American colonies. *This* origins story positions chattel slavery—the purchasing, selling, exchanging, branding, and torturing of Black people—as a precondition that facilitates the 1776 divorce from Great Britain.

This focus on 1619 does not ignore, as some critics of Jones sometimes accuse, that an African presence in Spanish Florida exists before 1619, the existence of Maroon communities, or the roles that African descendants played in exploring North American territories. Instead, it rightfully points to a decisive moment that placed Black people on a specific trajectory toward chattel slavery as the nation was birthed.

Jones, of course, has not been the first to offer this claim, but her *1619 Project* rapidly placed into the public and political spheres this conversation about slavery's enduring effects. It challenged directly attempts to deny slavery's brutality, the role anti-Black racism played in maintaining and perpetuating it, and how slavery's legacies matter now. Her project emerged in twenty-first-century political and cultural contexts that wanted to ban books like it. Detractors insisted that archives similar to Jones's, instead of clarifying and correcting dominant narratives, actually mis-told the truth about the United States' racial history and its legacies.

The economic exploitation of the enslaved Black population in the colonies, and soon to be in the United States, would in time make freedom from the tyranny of Great Britain a reality. Chattel slavery helped to enrich the country so that it could stand alone. The proliferation of slavery had occurred alongside the development of, as Jennifer Morgan puts it, "new cultural ideas about value, accounts, and trade," and this new valuation of human life operated on the notion of human fungibility. The exchange of Black human capital, like the Black people first traded, facilitated the birth and development of the nation. By turning attention to the roles that Black people—as human beings and commodities—played in laying the foundation for a declaration of independence, students of history develop a more comprehensive picture of Black people's long history in building the nation despite their exclusion from the full rights of citizenship.

There could be no exchange of human beings of one race for the profit of another without racism. Still, it may be difficult to ever know for certain whether racism inaugurates, precedes, or solidifies slavery, because racism, as the term circulates in the nineteenth and twentieth centuries, may not have originated as the anti-Black racist system that it quickly became. Yet ideas about difference, whether religious or racial, would later become racial. These ideas about race, in conjunction with increased demands for labor, certainly fueled the expansion and maintenance of slavery. That is, racialist and racist thinking bound the capitalist nation-building project that was thought to justify the enslavement and dehumanization of Black people. Justifications for enslavement often suggested that Black people's inherent, biologically determined inhumanity itself necessitated their enslavement. To sell Black people, they had to be first objectified. These ideas reflect the idea that had to be bridged: to exchange inanimate objects or other nonhuman beings as commodities is one practice; to reduce individuals who are clearly human, animate people into inanimate objects required curious logics and contradictory stretches of the imagination.

Through all of this, what were Black people thinking and feeling? How can we write history in a way that makes space for such a question? By placing the lived experiences—often through firsthand accounts—of enslaved people as their focus, studies of slavery and its legacies, now more than ever, attend to the importance of shifting the vantage point from which American history and culture get narrated. By foregrounding Black people and Black perspectives, they tell a more comprehensive and thorough story. They insist that focusing on a different and more diverse set of noteworthy events, people, and perspectives, from the history of America's birth and development, radically alters America's most popular and cherished stories about itself and its citizens. By tying America's founding to the colonies' first transaction in the transatlantic slave trade, for example, contemporary studies of slavery and its legacies centralize slavery, race, and racial-capitalism as a deeply connected triad that makes America's formation, development, and expansion possible. The story of these practices from the Black perspective is a key resource, as readers will see.

Slavery and racial hierarchies played crucial roles in both developing an early America *and* maintaining racial inequities and stratifications in the twenty-first century. Historians can no longer trivialize the ways that slavery, racism, and capitalism throughout history have coalesced to disenfranchise Black people while systematically advancing white people's and the nation's wealth and power. The contemporary study of slavery and its afterlife emphasizes an archive that unsettles dominant, popular, and sanitized representations of slavery. Such an archive can help citizens to develop clearer understandings of slavery's embeddedness in the nation's formation and continued development. *Black Narratives of Slavery: A Very Short Introduction* approaches slavery and its legacies by way of how Black people, Black culture, and Black cultural production have participated in this process of creating an archive from which to better understand and appreciate slavery's enduring impacts.

Narratives of slavery write and right representations of slavery

Black Narratives of Slavery uses the phrase "narratives of slavery" to capture a range of texts, films, writings, and transcribed dictation that enslaved and non-enslaved Black people have produced that articulate, reflect upon, and explore the historical and contemporary significance of North American chattel slavery. It demonstrates how analyzing the Black cultural productions that Black people have created during the past four centuries have aided in providing a more complete, fuller accounting of slavery and its legacies. While slavery exists in other parts of the diaspora, and non-Black people have (re)presented it, this volume locates its discussion in the context of the United States' chattel slavery and its legacies after Emancipation, and primarily focuses on Black people's engagement with them. Indeed, the autobiographical accounts of Black people enslaved during the nineteenth century—writing that traditionally has earned the moniker "slave narrative"—play an important role in this investigation, as do the stories that the enslaved and formerly enslaved "told" other people who recorded it for them (oral yet transcribed).

But the focus of this work extends beyond these important sources. The imaginative works of late twentieth-century fiction writers (post–civil rights narratives), the twenty-first-century cinematic representations of the peculiar institution, the writings of non-enslaved Black people who wrote during the nineteenth century, and more general writings about Black people's disenfranchisement after slavery until the present emerge among the sources that *Black Narratives of Slavery* examines as it charts out the long historical arc of slavery not only in the Black imagination and mind, but also in the American cultural and political fabrics. Black cultural producers and Black cultural production have emphasized the perspectives of Black people in exploring the meaningful and forceful ways slavery operated, mattered, and matters still.

Mainstream engagements with slavery in American culture continue to elide the perspectives of Black people by essentially whitewashing American history without acknowledging the white supremacy and anti-Black racism that propelled slavery and its legacies. This trend often relies on historical archives that reinforce the perspectives of the enslavers, and that, in the process, perpetuate the white supremacy and anti-Black racism that omit Black perspectives.

Chattel slavery was more than just an unfortunate epoch in American history; it was a lasting phenomenon with legacies that continue into the present. While this claim might seem self-evident to specialists or alert citizens who read carefully about slavery and its legacies, the ongoing attempts to ban books, critical race theory, Black studies courses and departments, or any discussion of race, gender, or sexuality exemplify why explicit cases must be made about the interrelationship between slavery, its enduring legacies, white supremacy, and anti-Black racism, and how they manifest themselves in everyday politics, conversation, and culture. To be clear, bans such as the ones just mentioned attempt to deny slavery's enduring legacies.

Black people's perspectives and experiences have brought into focus important, underappreciated, and yet insightful epistemologies about slavery and its legacies, and in the process have disrupted the ways that mainstream narratives try to usurp how slavery has been understood. Black-produced narratives of slavery collectively undermine the erroneous belief that Black people's points of view lack value, remain subordinate to those of white people, or are too subjective to be taken seriously; point out archival materials that explicitly or implicitly evidence Black people's thinking about the pre-life, life, and afterlife of slavery; emphasize the importance of Black perspectives and how they shape conversations and knowledges about slavery and its legacies; and consider how, in the absence of traditional written archival materials, imaginative works become their own archive that need examination.

America's *original sin—slavery*—continues to lurk in American cultural production, conversation, public policy, and public opinion. We can witness its enduring presence across American culture and politics, from Colson Whitehead's novel *The Underground Railroad* and Netflix's adaptation of Octavia Butler's novel *Kindred* to congressional bills proposed to study slavery and its impacts, a proposed bill for a commission to study slavery and its legacies in the state of Maryland, reparation initiatives in Evanston, Illinois, and debates about reparations in the state of California. These engagements with the enduring presence and

1. Dr. Charles H. Wright's International Afro-American Museum, which he founded in 1965, in Detroit, Michigan, celebrated and preserved African American history and culture. In nearby Chicago, the DuSable Museum had opened in 1961, and in Washington, DC, the Anacostia Community Museum would later open in 1967. They all prioritized Black perspectives in organizing and chronicling Black history and culture.

significance of slavery and its legacies mark moments that aim to diminish the impact of slavery's ongoing effects.

Black Narratives of Slavery conjoins a wide range of narratives of slavery across a broad historical period to understand not only how Black people, enslaved and not enslaved, have experienced or imagined slavery, but also how slavery's long reach—it's afterlife—has continued to shape Black life in the twenty-first century. Whereas the phrase "the life of slavery" refers to the historical period during which slavery remained legalized in the United States, "the afterlife of slavery" captures the eras following Emancipation when other legalized and extralegal means to terrorize and to disenfranchise Black people effectually reinstituted the principles, practices, and effects of slavery. In other words, by turning attention to the narratives produced during the last 200-plus years in particular, this volume examines American chattel slavery as a specific historical period that legally ended in 1865, and yet recognizes its impacts, effects, and significance as extending to the present day. Narratives of slavery tie the life of slavery and arguments to abolish it with the afterlife of slavery and arguments to stop its reconfigurations by way of Black Codes, Jim Crow segregation, and other forms of disenfranchisement.

Black Narratives of Slavery maintains that the *life* of slavery and *afterlife* of slavery depend on each other to make meaning. This codependent meaning-making claim guides how this book contextualizes and analyzes the narratives of slavery that it examines. As analytical and conceptual frameworks, the life of slavery and the afterlife of slavery bridge the past to the present to emphasize how nonlinear thinking remains an important framework for Black studies. When considered together, both of slavery's lives can also explain how different historical periods elucidate one another, and how they deepen one's understanding of the texts and the historical periods that witnessed their production and publication. The ongoing recovery of texts from earlier historical eras, the emergence of new scholarly perspectives and theoretical paradigms, and the curation of a more expansive Black archive of narratives of slavery reinforce the importance and usefulness of thinking about the life and afterlife of slavery simultaneously when examining narratives of slavery.

Slavery, in this context, becomes both the *precondition* for emancipation *and* the *postcondition* of emancipation, and inaugurates what Rinaldo Walcott refers to as the *long* emancipation. Emancipation was an unfinished project that unfolded gradually in the years following its legislation—indeed, descendants of slavery continue to do this work today. Similar to how the Emancipation Proclamation did not end slavery, but freed only the enslaved who resided in states that had seceded from the Union, Emancipation itself did not undo the cumulative effects of slavery or end its organizing principles or logics. Therefore, Emancipation is not over, and its beginning did not undo the material and psychic injuries that slavery has inflicted.

Black people have been keenly aware of the ongoing nature of Emancipation, and they have been recording, writing, documenting, and archiving it. We therefore can't study this ongoing process by organizing it into a straightforward timeline. Instead, this book identifies five types of *narratives of slavery* that focalize the perspectives, knowledges, and contributions of Black people to study slavery and its legacies. It classifies narratives into autobiographical narratives of slavery (slave narratives), oral yet transcribed narratives of slavery, Jim Crow narratives of slavery, post–civil rights era narratives of slavery (neo-slave narratives), and cinematic narratives of slavery. These descriptors in fact draw attention, in many ways, to how the past intrudes into the present, as well as how progress, freedom, and full citizenship rights often remain, in the words of the Harlem Renaissance poet Langston Hughes, "dreams deferred" that extend the work of the long emancipation.

Black Narratives of Slavery assumes the humanity of Black people. The formerly enslaved emerge as precisely that, formerly enslaved people, as opposed to slaves, the commodified objects. As people, the formerly enslaved maintain the position of historical agents whose history and culture begin prior to enslavement and whose personhood exists despite slavery's attempt to extinguish it. The analyses treat Black subjects as people whose perspectives, feelings, experiences, and knowledges matter. They also consider how Black people's ways of thinking and knowing inform how society understands slavery and its afterlives. Collectively, the narratives of slavery here, in addition to all of the other "work" they perform, provide access to a different degree of Black people's *interiority*—their psyches, their feelings, their psychological states, and their intimate knowledges—that often elude the archives (no records) and traditional slave narratives (omitted) to foreground Black material and ideological contributions to studies of slavery and its afterlives. Black cultural producers fill in the contemporary and historical gaps by using the historical record and imagining and filling in its omission and absences, similar to the process that Saidiya Hartman defines as "critical fabulation."

Autobiographical narratives of slavery have understandably dominated examinations of firsthand accounts of slavery. The late twentieth century witnessed a proliferation of neo-slave narratives from Black writers who had not lived during slavery, reimagining what slavery had been like from their standpoint after the civil rights movement. These twentieth-century works in turn increased engagement with slave narratives. While these two types of texts share important commonalities, the phrase *slave narratives* refers only to the former, whereas *neo-slave narratives* are fictional texts that (re)imagine slavery. While the phrase neo-slave narratives takes on a life of its own in light of the exponential production of said works of fiction after 1970, there exists an archive of nineteenth-century texts, that, in terms of their imaginative takes on slavery, could approximate the classification of neo-slave narratives, including Frederick

Douglass's *The Heroic Slave* (1853), Hannah Craft's *The Bondswoman's Narrative* (1861), and Martin Delany's *Blake, or the Huts of America* (1859). Here we can begin to see why it is important to look at categories of narratives of slavery that expand beyond straightforward chronology.

Free Black people writing against slavery: David Walker's *Appeal*

We find rich narratives of slavery in still more types of work. Non-enslaved Black thinkers, activists, and leaders during the nineteenth century often produced narratives of slavery, and their contributions to these debates demonstrate how slavery's reach extended into the wider body politic during the pre-emancipation and long-emancipation eras. Long before scholarly examinations of enslavement used the phrases "racial capitalism" or "anti-Black racism" to describe the racial and economic ideologies guiding the gendered and sexualized experiences that enslaved Black people endured, David Walker's *Appeal, in Four Articles* (1829) compellingly laid bare how capitalistic greed, animated by avarice, intersects with anti-Black racism to blight opportunities for advancement for enslaved Black people in particular, and for non-enslaved Black people more generally. Walker connects the experiences of enslaved Black people with those of non-enslaved Black people to show how, as a group, Black people experience second-class citizenship. Walker does not parallel the two groups' lack of rights to create a false equivalency between the specific disenfranchisement slavery makes possible for enslaved Black people and the general disenfranchisement that anti-Black racism made available to non-enslaved Black people, who, as a resonant example, decades later initially could not enlist in the military to fight in the Civil War. Rather, Walker instead clarifies how anti-Black racism infiltrates the entire nation and shapes race relations in the process. Walker provides what we would now call "a structural analysis" of anti-Black racism that examines Blackness as the ultimate sign of difference and analyzes how these ideas about racial differences are exploited in American chattel slavery.

In many ways, Walker's *Appeal* self-consciously tackles extant discourses that circulated in order to justify slavery as a natural and inevitable byproduct of racial difference. By casting Black people's degraded social positions as a consequence of their alleged *innate deficiencies*, pro-slavery arguments insisted that slavery was a benign institution designed to help Black people specifically and society more generally. According to these arguments, slavery remained necessary in order to save Black people from themselves as well as to *protect* white people from Black people. But, even more importantly, some also argued that were it not for slavery, Black people would return to their "natural" "savageries" from which slavery allegedly had rescued them. Yet Walker refutes the notion that natural inherent differences cause, explain, and justify Black people's unequal treatment in the United States or globally. If Black people are wretched, Walker explains that the depravation and degradation of slavery positions them in that condition.

In "Our Wretchedness in Consequence of Slavery," for example, Walker observes, "I know well, that there are some talents and learning among the coloured people of this country, which we have not a chance to develop, in consequence of our oppression; but our oppression ought not hinder us from acquiring all we can." Walker rejects pseudoscientific claims that characterized Blackness as an aberration that warranted subjugation. For Walker, racial essentialism—the belief that Black people have an inherent set of characteristics that are genetically or biologically determined—intentionally distorted the complex and systematized ways the United States' laws, public policies, attitudes, and norms promote and maintain slavery, anti-Black racism, and white supremacy. If given the same opportunities as white people, Black people would succeed and achieve,

Walker insists. On the one hand, Walker's refusal to let oppression "hinder us from acquiring all we can" recognizes the ubiquity of anti-Black racism and white supremacy as always threatening forces. On the other hand, he urges Black people to persist despite the best attempts to thwart their efforts.

More pointedly, pro-slavery arguments that relied on innate racial differences also misrepresented how capitalist greed further propelled anti-Black narratives to support slavery. Capitalism, or what Walker repeatedly refers to as avarice, partially explains why "the whites are dragging us around in chains and in handcuffs, to their new States and Territories to work their mines and farms, to enrich them and their children." Walker's focus on the present *and* the future demonstrates his awareness of how exploiting Black labor would have long-lasting effects. He emphasizes the role capitalist greed plays in slavery's intractability and pointedly undermines the notion that inherent Black inferiority drives the peculiar institution. By calling attention to capitalism's role, Walker suggests that white greed necessitates new explanations to justify the enslavement and dehumanization of Black people—"dragging us around in chains"; there is not anything inherent or essential to Blackness that calls for enslavement or second-class citizenship.

Walker's *Appeal* simultaneously gestures toward and refutes a barrage of sociological, economic, scientific, and religious discourses that had coalesced to justify enslavement. Walker's *Appeal* implores Black people (globally) to understand and reject their (abject) conditions; demands that Black people obtain their citizenship rights and opportunities to participate in society; urges white Christians in particular to recognize the contradiction between professing Christian faith and supporting slavery; demands the immediate end to slavery; and finally warns white Christians in particular, and white people more generally, of their impending destruction for failing to abolish slavery.

It is not happenstance that Walker's *Appeal* riffs on the Declaration of Independence and uses some of the literary conventions of the American Jeremiad to make his case. By invoking the Declaration of Independence, Walker turns attention to its paradoxical demand for freedom for white people even as it protected the enslavement of Black people. His *Appeal* offers a path toward freedom that liberates Black people from enslavement and white people from the white supremacy and anti-Black racism in which they invest to justify the disenfranchisement of Black people.

Walker's engagement with the paradoxes of freedom and enslavement that the Declaration of Independence underwrites shows how Black writers, activists, and thinkers have used these civic myths pre-Emancipation and throughout the long emancipation to emphasize the unfreedom of Black life, and to think about the sociopolitical changes required to grant Black people full citizenship rights. While Black writers, artists, and thinkers historically have pointed out the flawed aspects of the founding documents, and have identified the Constitution and its amendments as "myths" to the degree that they have marginalized or otherwise diminished Black people's rights, they, like Walker, also have asserted Black people's deservedness of the rights and protections these documents confer.

Although himself not enslaved, David Walker recognized the precariousness of his freedom, especially after the Fugitive Slave Act (1793) had further entangled racial and economic interests of even ordinary citizens. Slavery's presence threatened the freedom of any and every Black person any and everywhere. Although Northup himself did not pen *Twelve Years a Slave: Narrative of Solomon Northup, a Citizen of New York, Kidnapped in Washington City in 1841, and Rescued in 1853, from a Cotton Plantation Near the Red River in Louisiana*, Solomon Northup's experience shows that whether people were formerly enslaved or never enslaved, the presence of slavery made the threat of enslavement possible for *all* Black people. The legalization of "returning" self-emancipated or never-enslaved Black people to their *owners* (the Fugitive Slave Act of 1850), which financial rewards typically incentivized, underscored the tenuousness of Black freedom in a nation that upheld slavery.

While *Walker* takes great exception to anyone returning so-called fugitives, he holds a particular disdain for Black men who would capture and return their brethren. He acknowledges the ubiquity of this practice and insists that avarice once again prevails over the immorality of slavery. At the same time, this brutal law serves to subdue the development of a race consciousness among Black people that would stop Black men from aiding the Fugitive Slave Act—they choose self-interest over principle to survive, making them complicit with the same structures that oppress their fellow Black people. After Walker's death, the Supreme Court would later rule in *Dred Scott v. Sandford* (1857) that enslaved Black people's statuses as enslaved determined their fate; even if they traveled to a so-called free state or territory, they were to remain chattel. While the ruling itself was damning enough, Justice Taney's clarification in that ruling that Black men possessed "no rights which the white man was bound to respect" captured the heart of why Walker writes the *Appeal*; he demonstrates how anti-Black racism fuels slavery and reveals the embeddedness of these ideas in American politics and culture. If Black people, enslaved or not, were to become full citizens, these ideas, and the practices, customs, laws, and policies that reinforce them, would also need to be abolished.

While not the sole reason, this threat of enslavement during slavery, alongside the general existence of second-class citizenship and otherwise abridged rights, compelled non-enslaved Black people to campaign against slavery. Their non-autobiographical narratives of slavery take on slavery's systemic and individual encroachments on Black life and spell out how anti-Black racism affects the nation. The aftermath of slavery shows the prescience of pre-Emancipation narratives of slavery that anticipated the lingering and lasting impacts of slavery that would lie ahead. For just one example: post-Emancipation, formerly enslaved people found employment and housing by working as sharecroppers. While sharecropping purportedly *paid* Black people for *working* on the land of former owners, and *provided* them with housing, it in fact extended the economic exploitation of Black labor that slavery had made essential to impeding Black people's economic progress. In this and other ways, into the Jim Crow era and beyond, the ability to exploit emerged in the ways that slavery's legacies continued to shape American politics, society, and culture. While the concern with the interrelationship between anti-Black racism, capitalism, and slavery emerges in slave narratives and abolitionist texts, we can appreciate the early and powerful diagnoses of these problems in Walker's work.

Abolition, Emancipation, and the lingering problems with race

The so-called Negro Problem emerged in nineteenth-century debates about slavery as politicians, activists, abolitionists, and everyday white citizens asked themselves what to do with or about Black people. If Black people weren't enslaved, what would their role be? What limits could there be to keep them in check in a white supremacist world? In the popular and political imaginations, the presence of Black people, outside of the boundaries of slavery, challenged existing social hierarchies and assumed racial abilities, as well as ideas about who could access citizenship rights and handle citizens' responsibilities. Even those on the side of abolition couldn't see their way to total equality—at least not any time soon. The most popular abolitionist school of thought during the early part of the nineteenth century, gradualism, insisted on an eventual elimination of chattel slavery. Gradualism's resistance toward slavery hinged on its view of slavery as immoral, but it did not recognize the equality of races or want a freed Black population to disrupt white people's ways of life. Some gradualists were ideologically opposed to slavery, yet they still thought of Black people as racial "others" who, if given the opportunity to acquire freedom and literacy, would find themselves better off not in mainstream white American society.

Rather than advocating immediate racial equality or a world order to replace white supremacy, many gradualists looked to colonization as a solution. Their espousal of colonization efforts emerged in the context of the birth and the growth of the American Colonization Society (ACS). During the teen years of the nineteenth century, the ACS worked to *aid* free-born Black and newly emancipated (and formerly enslaved) Black people to move to Africa. Notably, colonization did not lie within a small sect of American political thinking, but rather manifested itself in some of the most influential political circles, and even had the support of President Lincoln.

In some ways, colonization movements pointed to the entrenchment and intractability of white supremacy and anti-Black racism: both forces remained so deeply embedded in and fundamental to America they would pose long-term obstacles to Black people achieving equality at home in America. Of course, this insight is not the one that pro-colonization advocates offered for exporting and separating Black people and further stealing their birthrights to the nation and its promises. Black activists such as Martin Delany rejected the pro-colonization premise that Black people are so biologically inferior or deficient that they could not assimilate into American society. To the contrary, he argued that Black people undoubtedly could assimilate and should claim their citizenship rights. He saw through what he called the "colonization scheme" to the deception at its core. Black people's rightful home is on the North American continent, he argued: "We are Americans, having a birthright citizenship—natural claims upon the country—claims common to all others of our fellow citizens—natural rights, which may, by virtue of unjust laws, be obstructed, but never can be annulled." Through its obstruction (unjust laws), slavery may have deferred the conferral of citizenship rights, but slavery itself could not deny the fact of Black people's personhood, their humanity, or the fact that they belonged in what Delany called "our country."

Black activists such as Delany produced narratives of slavery that thus played a significant role in rejecting both colonization and gradualism and in persuading white abolitionists, including William Lloyd Garrison, to also refuse colonization efforts. The Black influence on the rise of immediatism in abolitionist thinking cannot be underestimated; Black people lamented the stalled efforts of gradualism and compelled newly converted anti-colonization abolitionists to demand a quick end to slavery. Immediatists and Black activists understood that Emancipation would require a total reconstruction of society, including the removal of racial hierarchies. Because the movement of Reconstruction (1865–1877) failed to deliver a seemingly impossible goal, the life of slavery became its afterlife. A significant transformation to the social order and a radical dismantling of racial and economic hierarchies did not occur. The 1865 Emancipation of enslaved Black people consequently set off a long emancipation, which inaugurated a range of responses to the Negro Problem, but it did not engender a similar set of responses to the problems of white supremacy. Black cultural production, however, has kept a keen eye on the problem of white supremacy as it has pushed for Black people's full citizenship rights.

The contents of this volume

The continued constriction of Black people's rights and responsibilities after Emancipation finds life in the practices and logics of slavery, and maintains its afterlife in Jim Crow, its mutations, and the continued journey of the long emancipation, even after the modern civil rights movement. For this reason, *Black Narratives of Slavery* traces a historical trajectory that spans the seventeenth through twenty-first centuries. It examines narratives of slavery and connects the life and afterlives of slavery, while considering the simultaneous ways the texts under consideration help to think about the past, present, and future. After reading *Black Narratives of Slavery*, a reader will better appreciate how Black narratives of slavery include written and nonwritten texts that enslaved and non-enslaved people produced, often offer perspectives on slavery and its aftermath that challenge mainstream histories and historiographies, connect the life and afterlife of slavery to understand slavery's ongoing significance reject a linear narrative of American racial progress by foregrounding the interrelationship between the past and present, and complicate the genre of slave narratives by thinking about narratives of slavery.

Chapter 2
Autobiographical narratives of slavery

The phrase "autobiographical narrative of slavery" categorizes the autobiographical writings that formerly enslaved Black people wrote to demonstrate their *very* capacities to read and write, to detail the violent experiences they endured as enslaved Black people, to reveal the ways they acted against and within the constraints that slavery imposed upon them, to show what they endured to escape from slavery, and to offer a glimpse of their post-Emancipation lives following their escapes. As a specific type of autobiography, slave narratives incorporate, build upon, and revise the generic conventions of captivity, spiritual, and conversion narratives, alongside those of sentimental novels, as they chart the formerly enslaved moving from slavery to freedom.

While this chapter examines in particular the autobiographical narratives that formerly enslaved Black people wrote, autobiographical narratives of slavery also emerge in "as-told-to" narratives: narratives that Black people (formerly enslaved or free) dictated but someone else wrote down. Autobiographical narratives of slavery often address common themes like life prior to slavery's disruption of it, or their realization that they were in fact enslaved; the disruption of familial ties that slavery enacted; the physical violence that they and others in their communities experienced; their increasing desires for freedom and the

AUNT SALLY;

OR,

THE CROSS THE WAY OF FREEDOM.

A NARRATIVE OF THE SLAVE-LIFE AND PURCHASE OF THE MOTHER OF REV. ISAAC WILLIAMS, OF DETROIT, MICHIGAN.

"Thou shalt no more be termed Forsaken, ... for the Lord delighteth in thee."—ISAIAH lxii : 4.

CINCINNATI:

AMERICAN REFORM TRACT AND BOOK SOCIETY.

1858.

2. Title page of *Aunt Sally; or The Cross the Way of Freedom: A Narrative of the Slave-Life and Purchase of the Mother of Rev. Issaac Williams, of Detroit, Michigan*. This autobiographical narrative of slavery can be categorized into the "as-told-to" or "related to" or "dictated to" tradition in which the formerly enslaved does not write the narrative herself.

the idea that Black people lack that capacity to write, clarify that they are in fact the writers, and distinguish themselves from the "as-told-to" narratives of their peers. While editors and abolitionists did in fact assist the authors by providing editorial support, they did not in fact write the narratives nor offer any degree of written assistance that would call into question *who* really composed the narratives. At the same time, authors, editors, and abolitionists organized, marketed, and sold autobiographical narratives of slavery fully aware of the myriad questions that loomed about the authors' abilities to compose and masterfully organize such striking and compelling works, as well as the roles assisters played in the process.

Autobiographical narratives of slavery: Authenticating devices

Many of the autobiographical narratives of slavery contain prefaces (even ones the authors themselves wrote), notes from an editor, or an editorial introduction, all of which function to help verify, or, *authenticate* the narratives. These *authenticating devices* or *authenticating documents* serve several purposes for both the narratives themselves and society at large, and their location in the texts matters too. Structurally, authenticating devices and documents typically (although not always) appear *before* the actual narrative begins. Collectively, authenticating devices assist in verifying the author's identity, emphasizing the author's authorship, confirming the author's enslavement and escape, attesting to the truthfulness of the narrative, denying any exaggeration of details, reiterating the importance of abolishing slavery, and acknowledging the editor's own limited role in shaping the narrative.

The institution of slavery and fierce debates about abolition further explain why the authenticating devices and documents emerge in the written narratives. The very production of autobiographical narratives of slavery, for example, undercut

Great Chain of Being theories that had denied Black humanity and further justified the racial and racist discourses supporting slavery. White populations found themselves in disbelief about Black people's capacity to produce the narratives. In this context, the authenticating documents point to the *incredulity* of white people at Black people's capacities more so than to an *incredibility* of Black production. During slavery, enslaved Black people believed that literacy was a key tool they could use to gain and maintain freedom, and, in many instances, to prove their humanity.

Authenticating devices in autobiographical narratives of slavery orient and introduce readers to the narratives so their locations in the narrative can matter. Authors and editors had to negotiate how not to privilege the editorial voice and concurrently attract and persuade a reader. Literary critics and historians have raised this issue, among others, in their investigation of autobiographical narratives of slavery. When an editor's note, for example, precedes the author's preface, introduction, or first chapter, it may unintentionally overshadow the formerly enslaved person's own story. This subordination would reinforce the very types of social and racial hierarchies that slavery demanded and that the autobiographical narratives of slavery worked against. Throughout autobiographical narratives of slavery, the degree of authentication within a narrative varies, as does how authors implicitly and explicitly respond to incorporate or even self-authenticate alongside the devices.

The dialogue between authenticating devices, self-authentication, and the autobiographical narratives of slavery themselves sets forth important contexts for understanding the conditions of slavery, the authorship of texts, and the reception of the texts and the authors. Authors themselves, either in their own prefaces or throughout the narratives, explain any perceived deficiencies in their narratives as a consequence of slavery and its forbidding of their learning to read or write. Having mastered literacy so late in life, and having endured slavery, the authors of the autobiographical narratives of slavery call attention to the magnanimity of the feat of writing the narrative. Slavery thus becomes the cause and effect of any deficiency and not the author's supposed biological inferiority. The fact that they are writing a narrative already undermines the premise of Black inferiority and incapability, but by including these ideas the authors also turn attention to their persistence: Black people continue to face them even after accomplishing that which was thought they could not.

In Harriet Jacobs's *Incidents in the Life of a Slave Girl, Written by Herself*, the author's own preface *precedes* Lydia Maria Child's editorial introduction, yet both the preface and introduction work simultaneously to reinforce Jacobs's authorship, to note Child's limited editorial role, and to indict slavery for encroaching upon Black people's rights. By placing Jacobs's own preface first, *Incidents* foregrounds and maintains Jacobs's role in producing, guiding, and determining the incidents from her life that merit disclosure, consideration, and evaluation. In the author's preface, for instance, Jacobs asks for forgiveness, noting "I wish I were more competent to the task I have undertaken. But I trust my readers will excuse deficiencies in consideration of circumstances. I was born and reared in Slavery." Jacobs correlates her "deficiencies" with her "circumstances" to emphasize that the conditions of chattel slavery prevent Black people from achieving, and, in the process, adds to the chorus of Black people who refute the idea that Black people are biologically inferior to white people.

In Lydia Maria Child's introduction, she also confirms Jacobs's role in independently writing the text by emphasizing her own limited editorial role. Child explains: "At [Jacobs's] request, I have revised the manuscript; but such changes as I have made have been made mainly for purposes of condensation and orderly arrangement. I have not added any thing to the incidents, or changed the import of her very pertinent remarks. With trifling exceptions, both the ideas and language are her own." If Jacobs trusts readers' abilities to read complexly and understand the layered meanings in the text, and to forgive her alleged deficiencies, and if readers trust Child's limited role, readers can also consider another layer of Jacobs's trust: that she imagines a reading public who will also grasp the irony of her humility—that someone reared in slavery could produce such a well-crafted tale—and understand how her sisters still in bondage could similarly achieve, if the reading public unites to demand the abolition of slavery. The preface, introduction, and story then work together to achieve this goal.

For all the discussion about the autobiographical narratives of slavery's political and sociocultural value and usages, it is important not to over overlook or underappreciate the literary craft, rhetorical ingenuity, and literary mastery that the autobiographical narratives of slavery evidence. Their aesthetic innovations notably shifted and set the stage for subsequent Black American literature and what has come to be known as a Black American literary tradition. On the one hand, readers demanded an unembellished and unadulterated truth. On the other, authors recognized their roles in creating a *literary* work. Thus, the autobiographical narratives of slavery themselves resist a "sociological realism" of an unembellished and unadulterated truth. Content and form bridge aesthetic and political interests and thus cooperate to advance a literary tradition and a quest for Black people's rights.

An additional profundity of the autobiographical narratives of slavery emerges in their consistent abilities to anticipate, respond to, and leverage the critiques that readers might offer against them to instead further their mission to abolish slavery and secure for Black people access to their citizenship rights. From sympathizers to antagonists, from abolitionists to proponents of slavery, from northern readers to southern ones, from Christians who enslaved Africans to those who wanted to free them, from formerly enslaved Black people to free Black people who knew only the threat of slavery, from white people who were against slavery yet believed Black people to be inferior to white people (if they believed them to be people at all) to white people who recognized Black people's humanity and supported equal rights, these potential readers of the autobiographical narratives of slavery would bring a wide range of ideologies, feelings, and opinions about the peculiar institution. In trying to persuade readers, the formerly enslaved needed to be ever conscious of these varying readers.

The diversity of types of readers of these narratives, to whom the writers had to address themselves, and hope to win over—regardless of their political beliefs—in turn emblematized the broader conversations and disputes within society as a whole about race, slavery, and rights. Writers had to anticipate how their stories would resonate with each of these publics when they published such works. With their own contested political status and questioned humanity, the formerly enslaved entered and shaped debates about Black people, Black life, and Black freedom that persist into the twenty-first century. Key examples of the autobiographical narrative of slavery can help us to further understand slavery and its afterlives.

Written by himself: Frederick Douglass's first narrative

Through his speeches, essays, fiction, and autobiographies, Frederick Douglass, a renowned speaker, champion for Black civil rights, and vociferous critic of anti-Black racism, was one of the most prolific Black writers and activists. Douglass wrote and published three autobiographical narratives of slavery: *Narrative of the Life of Frederick Douglass, an American Slave, Written by Himself* (1845), *My Bondage and My Freedom* (1855), and *Life and Times of Frederick Douglass* (1881). Collectively, Douglass's narratives explain how slavery's anti-Black racism and mechanisms of social control and exploitation operate during and after slavery, and thus demonstrate how slavery's lives and afterlives connect. That is, the three autobiographies show how slavery eclipses Black life and opportunities during slavery (*Narrative*), how even in Douglass's personal freedom the threats of enslavement always lurk (*Bondage*), and how the legacies of slavery continue to thwart Black freedom in the post-Emancipation era (*Life*). *Narrative*, nonetheless, has remained his most iconic autobiographical writing, and part of this iconicity (and canonicity) relates to its position in American letters and history as one of the most widely engaged autobiographical narratives of slavery. The prominence of the text is also in part due to Douglass's own towering stature in Black politics and life during the nineteenth century. While important, we can't take Douglass's *Narrative* as a stand-in for all works of this genre. Still, as part of an introductory study of the autobiographical narrative of slavery, it is worthwhile to spend time examining the salient issues that Douglass illuminates. We can also glean useful interpretive strategies from spending time with this famous text—strategies we can then apply to the diverse body of autobiographical narratives of slavery.

Narrative of the Life uses many of conventions found in autobiographical narratives of slavery. Douglass includes prefaces from both famed abolitionist William Lloyd Garrison and lawyer Wendell Phillips that function just as much, if not more, to bolster Douglass's accounting as they do to serve the other typical roles authenticating devices play. Garrison's preface emphasizes Douglass's rhetorical eloquence in his anti-slavery speeches, and Garrison points to those speeches as evidence of Black potential and achievement in the absence of slavery. Whereas Garrison's preface pointedly focuses on Douglass's role as an abolitionist, and connects his rhetorical eloquence with his written agility, Phillips's preface similarly exalts the richness of the written *Narrative*. By casting Douglass as one of "the lions [who] wrote history," Phillips underscores the importance and urgency of the (formerly) enslaved man writing this history of enslavement as a way to disrupt the master narratives that portrayed slavery as a *benign* institution and underestimated its savagery, brutality, and immorality.

Although both of these prefaces precede Douglass's voice in the narrative, Douglass's title itself first grounds his voice in a very specific way, as he contrasts the "written by himself" with "an American slave" and the "American" with "slave." Whereas the titular juxtaposition—"American slave"—exposes the hypocrisy of America championing freedom while enslaving Black people, the juxtaposition of "written by himself" and "an American slave" calls attention to his literacy despite pro-slavery arguments that deny the possibility. Douglass and other writers find different ways to self-authenticate even as they get authenticated. Both processes work together and inform how readers receive and interpret the texts.

Divided into eleven chapters, and including an appendix that specifically addresses Douglass's criticism of the religious practices of white people who enslaved Black people, *Narrative* captures significant moments in Douglass's life that elucidate slavery's horrors, animate his desire for freedom, and conclude in his freedom and eventual marriage. In many ways, Douglass labors to show *both*, in his own words, "how a man was made a slave [*and*] how a slave was made a man." A host of themes and concerns animate *Narrative of the Life* as Douglass recalls the triumphs, disappointments, fights, cunnings, casual and systemic anti-Black racism, Christian hypocrisy, quotidian violence, sorrow, despair, and hope that characterized his life as an enslaved Black man residing in Maryland. Significantly, much of the narrative arc invites an examination of how Douglass constructs his quest for freedom as a simultaneous quest for Black manhood that requires literacy, financial independence, and a rejection the Christian hypocrisy of the slaveholding South. This triad of concerns binds the narrative and becomes the framework through which readers gain understanding of the intersecting concerns Douglass brings to bear. Similar themes and topics emerge across a large swath of autobiographical narratives of slavery. For example, Douglass begins his story by charting his own genealogy and simultaneously writing himself into history.

This writing into history remains particularly noteworthy because it turns immediate attention to how slavery had deprived him of the normal, state-issued documents that serve a similar purpose—for example, a birth certificate. Emphasizing his previous status as chattel, Douglass relates: "I have no accurate knowledge of my age, never having seen any authentic record containing it." The absence of a birth certificate signals for Douglass the ways that slavery profoundly disrupts Black familial relationships; not only does he not know his age, but he only knows rumors of whom his father may be. Without birth certificates, neither the enslaved nor their parents (particularly if both were Black and enslaved) possessed any legal claims to their own personhood or their children's *or* the legal and civil rights that personhood bestows.

In attuning the reader to this fact in the narrative's opening lines, Douglass reminds the reader that from denying basic individual civil rights—such as being able to obtain a birth certificate—to more communal civil rights—such as being able to keep one's family intact—slavery provides a wide pathway for Black civic exclusion. By referring to himself, his family, and the many others whom he has encountered to evidence his claims, Douglass contends that, in this respect, his experiences reflect those of the masses of enslaved Black people. He also points out early on that slavery's infringement on Black people's rights remains pervasive, systemic, and quotidian. Black people become the subject matter experts on slavery's pernicious effects on Black life, and their insights counter the paternalistic perspective of owners that slavery is benign or otherwise helpful for Black people.

Douglass on literacy

In recalling his own quest to attain literacy, Douglass suggests that states enacted anti-literacy laws to reinforce slavery's power, and that, instead of diminishing enslaved Black people's interest in learning how to read, anti-literacy laws amplify their desire. Owners had a vested interest in maintaining Black people's illiteracy, particularly as global revolts against slavery increased, free Black people and abolitionists alike published more writings and pamphlets that condemned slavery, and literate Black people and other allies rejected biblical interpretations of slavery as a God-ordained institution to which Black people needed to acquiesce. Douglass appreciates the importance of literacy when Douglass's owner, Mr. Auld, chastises his wife, Mrs. Auld, for teaching Douglass how to read. In a somewhat ironically prophetic declaration, Mr. Auld insists, "If you give a nigger an inch, he will take an ell. A nigger should know nothing but to obey his master—to do as he is told to do. Learning would *spoil* the best nigger in the world. Now, if you teach that nigger how to read, there would be no keeping him. It would forever unfit him to be a slave." Auld believes that the "inch" would open the door to a wider "ell" and provide a path for Douglass to want even more freedoms, as Douglass eventually does.

Given that in 1831 Nat Turner had organized a protest (slave rebellion), and a host of southern states enacted anti-literacy laws that impacted free and enslaved Black people (Virginia in 1831, Alabama in 1833), it is not surprising that Auld, and other owners, took exception to teaching the enslaved how to read; by reading the Bible for themselves, for example, Black preachers, leaders, and activists had been able to challenge biblical justifications of enslavement and instead identify a biblical narrative of freedom. Auld essentially contends that learning would *spoil* Douglass because literacy would open up the possibility for Douglass to gain access to troves of writings that contradicted pro-slavery arguments about Blackness, slavery, freedom, religion, and natural rights upon which slavery relied (e.g., David Walker's *Appeal*).

If, as Auld suggests, and Douglass understands, the learned self *becomes* (more) incompatible with enslavement, learning or literacy emerges as foundational in slavery's undoing. Any tool, let alone this specific one, that "would forever unfit him" Douglass seeks as he grasps the implications of Auld's warning. Douglass soon after confides: "These words sank deep in my heart, stirred up sentiments within that lay slumbering. . . . I now understood the white man's power to enslave the Black man. . . . From that moment, I now understood the pathway from slavery to freedom." Invigorating his mission to learn how to read, Douglass taps into the broader cultural sentiment that Black people lacked the capacity to read, and learned how to read *and* to write. In other words, he, like other enslaved Black people who learned to formally read and write, resisted the oppression that anti-literacy laws or practices had added to slavery's denial of rights for Black people. Strategically and with his characteristic ingenuity, Douglass *encourages* young white boys to teach him how to write by challenging them to write more than the words he knew how to read or write at that time. Through this game, Douglass added immensely to his written vocabulary.

The ways Douglass learned how to read and to write and the passing of anti-literacy laws point to the fundamental contradictory and tenuous yet pervasive logics in slavery. If Black people lacked the capacity to learn to read and to write, both anti-literacy laws and word-spelling games would be unnecessary. This parallel again points to the multipronged attacks against pro-slavery arguments that Douglass levels. It also demonstrates the impetus of his drive to learn how to read and the lengths through which he would go to do so. Douglass's thirst for literacy and knowledge, and his determination to achieve these goals, illuminate a larger pattern in both autobiographical narratives of slavery and society more broadly, where Black people emphasize their interest in learning, and show, once given the opportunity, how they use it and flourish by it.

Douglass on slavery and Christianity

The Second Great Awakening invigorated abolitionist arguments against slavery as abolitionists began to emphasize slavery's immorality and contrariness to God's will. While this increased anti-slavery sentiment did not always translate into a belief in Black people's equality, it did provide a pathway for building coalitions to overthrow slavery. This context shapes Douglass's engagement with religion, as he, similar to David Walker, takes special care to demonstrate for the reader the ways that slavery, as an institution, and owners of the enslaved, as implementers of the institution's violence, run afoul of *true* or *pure* Christianity. Douglass does not mince any words when he insists that the Christianity of the slaveholding South is by no means Christianity. Throughout the chapters, Douglass recalls frequent incidents where he describes *self-professed* Christians as orchestrating the most brutal enactments of physical violence against the enslaved, as well as how Christian conversion increases (rather than decreases) this inhumaneness.

Discussing one master's Christianity, Douglass laments: "If it had any effect on his character, it made him more cruel and hateful in all his ways; for I believe him to have been a much worse man after his conversion than before. Prior to his conversion, he relied upon his own depravity to shield and sustain him in his savage barbarity; but after his conversion, he found religious sanction and support for his slaveholding cruelty." For Douglass, the danger of this form of Christianity—what makes it impure—is that its pro-slavery logics and justifications ignore a broader, more pervasive narrative arc toward freedom and liberation. Many Black interpretations of Christianity, including several of the Black American spirituals that circulate in American culture alongside the autobiographical narratives of slavery, demonstrate a strong belief that unfreedom goes against the freedoms that biblical narratives champion. Given Black people's enslaved status, biblical narratives in which God (or Jesus) sided with or liberated oppressed, disempowered, or disenfranchised people resonated with them.

Because Douglass unflinchingly turns our attention to the pervasive perversions of pure Christianity throughout *Narrative*, he adds an appendix in which he clarifies his position about Christianity, citing specific examples of enslavement practices that defy biblical principles, and asks the reader one final time to join the abolitionist cause. He does so to assure the readership that his criticisms function to clarify, not blaspheme; he wants to persuade them even more in joining his calls to abolish slavery. Significantly, Douglass's appendix understands the centrality of Christian readers as a part of his wide readership, and acknowledges that in order to persuade he cannot offend.

Douglass's *Narrative of the Life*, alongside his speeches on the abolitionist circuit, reinforces his status as a prolific abolitionist whose autobiographical narratives of slavery—written and oral—recount the horrors of slavery, announce how enslaved Black people managed to circumvent some of slavery's constrictions to form relationships and community, and persuade readers and listeners to abolish slavery. While Douglass's narratives include the experiences of others, the tales remain primarily autobiographical. His identity as a man shapes his perspectives and the contours of his enslavement. To make this point and to better understand the specific experiences of enslaved Black women, scholars and other interested people have turned to the autobiographical narratives of slavery that formerly enslaved Black women produced. In particular, Harriet Jacobs's *Incidents in the Life of a Slave Girl* has become a paradigmatic and representative text for understanding the particular experiences of Black womanhood during enslavement and how the ideas she expresses resonate in the long emancipation, during slavery's afterlife.

Incidents in the Life

Harriet Jacobs's iconic *Incidents in the Life of a Slave Girl, Written by Herself* (1861) chronicles pivotal moments in the life of Linda Brent (Jacobs's pseudonym) as she moves from slavery to freedom. Throughout this journey, Jacobs increasingly understands how her gender and status as a mother complicate her quest for liberation. Calling upon the readers' emotions as sentimental novels do, Jacobs blends and innovates the conventions of the autobiographical narrative of slavery and sentimental novel genres. Through them, Jacobs articulates a harrowing and clever story that accentuates the ways that ideas about race, gender, and sexuality intersect to make Black women especially vulnerable to the sexual violence that the institution sanctions. From her initial realization of her status as chattel, to the sexual harassment she experiences at the onset of puberty, to the lack of compassion she endures from her jealous mistress, to her decision to have sex out of wedlock with a man *she chooses*, to her choice to remain in her "loophole of retreat" for approximately seven years to escape her owner's sexual harassment *and* remain near her children, to her final escape and ultimate agreement to let someone purchase her freedom, Jacobs's desires for sexual and bodily autonomy propel the narrative's arc.

Published during the height of the anti-slavery movement, *Incidents* works to expand support for abolition through its readership, as Jacobs, dissimilar from Douglass, does not find herself as part of a larger anti-slavery network that also allows her to advance her narrative of slavery on the abolitionist lecture circuit. Moreover, Jacobs remains deeply invested in showcasing the plight of Black women because, as Shateema Threadcraft points out in *Intimate Justice*, "[t]he sexual, reproductive, and caretaking coercion and exploitation within the slave system was a burden that fell almost exclusively on enslaved women," and

Harriet Jacobs in 1894.

3. Harriet Jacobs, whose pseudonym was Linda Brent when she wrote *Incidents in the Life of a Slave Girl, Written by Herself*, was born in 1813 in Edenton, North Carolina, and died on March 7, 1897, in Washington, DC. She is buried in Mount Auburn Cemetery in Cambridge, Massachusetts.

because "whites exercised considerable power over enslaved women's capacities for reproduction, nurture, and care in a manner not typically experienced by Black men." Indeed, some of the most detailed recollections that Jacobs shares focus on sexual harassment, intimidation, and coercion; her compromised ability to care for her children and her parents' to care for theirs; and the actions she takes to undo or blunt the effects of slavery. In a profound moment in the text, Jacobs underscores her agency by noting that "my master had power and law on his side; I had a determined will. There is might in each." By focusing on incidents that highlight the sexual dimensions of slavery for Black women, and the behaviors she uses to free herself from their *absolute* control—to show the might of her will—Jacobs homes her audience to that of white women in the North who she hopes can understand and empathize with Black women's plights and become inspired to support slavery's abolition.

Because of *Incidents*' examination of the multidimensionality of race, gender, and sexuality, Black feminists have claimed Jacobs and *Incidents* as a foremother and fore-text, respectively, of Black feminist theory and practice. Well before academic scholarship introduced the phrases "double consciousness" (Frances Beale), "multiple jeopardy" (Deborah King), "womanism" (Alice Walker), or "interlocking oppressions" (Patricia Hill Collins) to articulate the specific ways that gender and sexuality inflect Black women's experiences of racial discrimination and racial disenfranchisement, Black women writers were articulating these concepts, ideas, and frameworks in their writing as they thought about Black people's oppression *and* freedom. Within the body of autobiographical narratives of slavery that Black women penned, *Incidents* maintains a paradigmatic role in showcasing Black women's specific experiences of oppression and, as importantly, how they resisted it to carve paths toward liberation. Jacobs and *Incidents* remain a key figure and text, respectively, in Black feminist thinking about Black feminism, Black women's resistance, and Black liberation.

Divided into forty-one chapters, excluding the preface and the appendix (which contains endorsements from white community members), *Incidents* initially focuses on the earlier years of Jacobs's life to demonstrate how her family maintained bonds despite slavery's ability to alter familial relationships through sales and other disruptive practices, how a Christian mistress had taught her how to read and to write (perhaps not perceiving her as much of a threat because of her gender), how quotidian acts of violence from Christian owners marked everyday life for the enslaved, how she and her family bonded to develop insights into the hypocrisy and flaws of the peculiar institution, how her parents and grandmother worked to instill morals in her and her brother, and how the institution of slavery tried to undermine and compromise those morals despite their best efforts to uphold them.

While the first four chapters of the narrative point toward some of the generic ways that slavery impacts enslaved life, chapter 5 marks a significant turning point in *Incidents*—a move from the general to the specific. Jacobs indeed abhors the facts that slavery does not recognize or honor the enslaved people's familial units and that owners often reneged on promises they made to grant enslaved people freedom. But that hatred becomes vitriol when the onset of puberty introduces her to a new world of harassment and gamesmanship that directly encroach upon her freedom and simultaneously invigorate her desire for it. In other words, what Jacobs describes as "the trials of girlhood," the multitude of unwanted (and unnatural) sexual overtures from owners that enslaved Black girls experience as a consequence of their (natural) sexual maturation, anticipate, structure, and guide Jacobs's journey toward freedom and desire for abolition.

Jacobs on Black women's bodily autonomy

Jacobs upends the characterization of Black women and girls as Jezebels by instead casting them as vulnerable subjects unprotected from the unchecked sexual power and lasciviousness of white owners. The stereotype of the Jezebel emerges during slavery and functions to rationalize the rape of Black women by characterizing them as hypersexual, insatiable, and therefore unable to be raped. As such, Black women must be controlled and their libidos subdued. *Incidents* turns this image upside down by highlighting how the institution of slavery facilitates white men's abilities to rape and harass Black girls and women. In addition to oversexualizing Black women, slavery desexualizes white men and denies Black women legal remedies for their sexual exploitation. Patriarchy and racial domination reinforce each other on the plantation and inhibit white women from forming alliances with enslaved Black women and girls to challenge either system.

Jacobs notes that both age and perceived beauty complicate the enslaved Black girls' lives by making them both more attractive to the owner and hated by his wife, thus facilitating the harassment and inhibiting any protections. Jacobs recalls "If God has bestowed beauty on her, it will prove her greatest curse. That which commands admiration in the white woman only hastens the degradation in the female slave. . . . My master met me at every turn, reminding me that I belonged to him, and swearing by heaven and earth that he would compel me to submit to him." Jacobs's comment in chapter ten remains instructive because it identifies how the confluence of ideas about race, gender, and sexuality that protects and exalts white womanhood invites an assault on Black womanhood. It also, in the process, acknowledges Black girls' and Black women's subjectivity and insists that they deserve similar protections. She rejects this double racial standard of womanhood and uses it as the entry point to make her case against slavery's specific cruelties to Black women.

During the nineteenth century, the cult of true womanhood provided a set of ideals to which "true" women could aspire, and *Incidents* embeds Jacobs's awareness of these ideals when she addresses her primary audience. Jacobs provides numerous examples of her attempts to achieve or maintain this ideal: piety (moral rectitude), submissiveness (subservience to husband), domesticity (head of household affairs), and purity (virginity until marriage). Jacobs explains her inability to uphold these ideals as a consequence of the circumstances of slavery and not because Black women inherently lack the ability do so. The images of her owner pursuing her and attempting to prevent her from choosing her own lover or husband place slavery's inhumanity under greater scrutiny by showing the pains she goes through to maintain autonomy over her body. Jacobs labors to show that she, and by extension, other enslaved Black women, desire to live up to these expectations but for the fact that slavery stops her and them at every turn.

In a particularly celebrated passage, Jacobs *chooses* to have sex with her preferred lover, Mr. Sands, rather than endure rape by her owner, Dr. Flint, or his attempts to *give her* to a man she does not desire. Afterwards, Jacobs invites the reader to forgive her, writing:

> But, O ye happy women, whose purity has been sheltered from childhood, who have been free to choose the objects of your affection, whose homes are protected by law, do not judge the poor desolate slave girl too severely! If slavery had been abolished, I, also could have married the man of my choice; I could have had a home shielded by laws; and I should have been spared the painful task of confessing what I am now about to relate.

In many ways, this passage drives Jacobs's inability to achieve true womanhood, and the contrast between free women of the North and enslaved women fuels her request for white women to join the abolition movement. Whereas white women have protection of their virginity from childhood, enslaved Black women experience "the trials of girlhood" as they age and are thought to become more sexually available. Whereas white women can choose a husband to marry, Black women cannot legally marry even if they choose their lover. Whereas white women have customs to protect their domestic spaces, enslaved Black women do not possess similar rights. Whereas white women can be moral exemplars and practice Christian principles, slavery compromises enslaved Black women's abilities to do so equally. By using the contrasting sociopolitical circumstances to show why Black women and white women cannot be held to the same standards, Jacobs simultaneously calls for an abolition of slavery in order to make enslaved Black women's aspirations toward the cult of true womanhood actually achievable.

Although Jacobs ultimately agrees to let Mrs. Bruce purchase her freedom, her narrative ends by pointing to the ways that slavery's stains remain around her. In freedom, Jacobs laments in the final chapter that her narrative ends in "freedom" and not in the usual way of marriage. On the one hand, this juxtaposition again emphasizes the differences between white women's lives and enslaved and free Black women's lives. On the other hand, it invites the reader to question whether marriage provides freedom—the two resolutions juxtaposed. More to the point, Jacobs further calls into question what freedom will mean for others and herself in light of their "previous condition" as enslaved "chattel." Although she has not become financially destitute, she does experience financial hardships; she writes to sway abolition *and* to earn money. Jacobs ultimately invites readers to consider what post-Emancipation life will look like and what challenges the formerly enslaved will endure. Jacobs's ending presages the challenges the nation will face after Emancipation, and the questions about what Black freedom looks like will continue to animate narratives of slavery for decades to follow. The enduring legacy of Harriet Jacobs cannot be underestimated.

As a genre, the autobiographical narrative of slavery exhibits many complexities. It includes various subgenres, only some of which the examples of Douglass and Jacobs represent. Some of the as-told-to narratives, for example, had white editors, whereas others had black ones: this matters, as the editor's race may have shaped the narratives' content. Other narratives, like that of Henry Box Brown, initially were labeled "as-told-to" but then re-emerged as "written-by-self." Autobiographical narratives of slavery are as heterogeneous as the lives of their authors, varied still more by their diverse paths to publication. This variety shapes the care with which one has to approach the commonalities and specifics of the genre.

Chapter 3
Not written by themselves: Oral yet recorded narratives of slavery

Born Isabella Baumfree and enslaved in New York until 1826, Sojourner Truth gave a legendary speech at the Women's Rights Convention (1851) in Akron, Ohio, that thrust her into prominence in the nation's literary and cultural imaginations. In an impromptu speech, Truth reportedly riled attendees to support women's suffrage. Truth's core argument defies contemporary anti-suffrage logics that excluded Black and white women from the right to vote. Through a series of contrasts that rely on her experiences as a formerly enslaved Black woman, Truth essentially refutes the underlying premise that biology has made women physically and intellectually weak and therefore doubly unqualified to exercise the right to vote. And, by acknowledging her own identity as both a Black person and a woman while making this argument, she shows that not only white women deserve the rights under discussion—Black women are women, too, and what's right for womankind should extend to her. For her, these two identities do not contradict each other, and her rhetorical statement, "I am a Woman," or the rhetorical question often (and perhaps erroneously) attributed to her, "Arn't I a woman?," emphasizes this point. Truth's speech turns attention to the parallel ways that biological essentialism functions to deny rights to both Black people and white women. While some suffragists reportedly did not want the comingling of the "woman" question alongside the "race" question, Truth's speech adds to the chorus of Black women showing the inseparability of race and gender for Black women's personal and political identities.

An attendee at the convention, Frances Gage popularized a transcribed version of Truth's speech, titled "Arn't I a Woman?," and it was this version that was taken up by the cultural imagination and mythologized. But Gage's transcription seems unlikely attributable to Truth—Truth's age, birthplace, and place of residence all clash with aspects of Gage's version. Gage's recollection and representation of Truth's word choices seemingly caricature southern (enslaved) Black speech patterns, but Truth herself did not have a southern accent, nor did she speak with a southern dialect. Fortunately, this is not the only written record we have of Truth. In *Narrative of Sojourner Truth* (1881), Truth's amanuensis reports Truth's difficulty in communicating with one set of owners because she spoke *Dutch* and they spoke English. So why would a Dutch-speaking enslaved Black woman living in New York mimic certain speech patterns that may emerge more prominently in the American South? Most likely, Gage exaggerated for effect, which calls other aspects of her transcription into question.

The recovery and archival work of Black feminist scholars has all but corroborated the fact that Truth did not give the *exact* speech that Gage attributes to her, even though elements of the speech that she gave do emerge in Gage's representation. While we can't trust the Gage text in its diction or all of its substance, the powerful overall message of the speech still speaks to us through history.

Furthermore, we can learn from the misrepresentations of Truth in Gage's text. Specifically, Gage's depiction of Truth using a southern dialect makes two important points, with lessons that apply more broadly in the study of narratives of slavery—particularly texts not constructed by their own Black subjects, representing Black people's thoughts. First, this stylistic

4. Sojourner Truth remained a vigilant anti-slavery and women's rights advocate, and found herself among her contemporaries, including Angelina and Sarah Grimke, Frederick Douglass, and Henry Highland Garnet, all of whom played significant roles in the quests for Black freedom.

choice by Gage to caricature Truth's language reminds us that the era conjoined casual anti-Black racism—even among anti-slavery sympathizers—with white supremacist anti-Black racism. Both of these phenomena shaped how white people thought of, imagined, and represented Black life, thought, and feelings. Second, however problematic these representations prove to be, they can also reveal important insights into Black people's thinking—it would be a mistake to completely dismiss Gage's transcription despite the racist choice on her behalf. In the case of the latter, analyses must bear in mind how anti-Black racism mediates the production, circulation, and reception of the representation. By focusing primarily on the written-by-the-self narratives of slavery, scholars and readers would overlook important *oral* and *as-told-to yet recorded* traditions that emerge at the beginning of African American literary tradition's formalization and persist throughout. On the one hand, it remains true that those who wrote their own accounts were sending a political message by doing so. On the other hand, some African American thinkers, activists, and cultural producers had only editorial (or editing) processes available to preserve and transmit their narratives of slavery to challenge racial ideologies, and they, too, deserve consideration even as analyses take into account how their recorders or representors may have embedded their own racist ideologies in the recording.

Formerly enslaved African Americans such as Frederick Douglass, Harriet Jacobs, Elizabeth Keckley, James W. C. Pennington, Henry Box Brown, and more than a hundred others who wrote about their own enslavement grappled with questions they knew their autobiographical narratives of slavery would raise. Would readers believe the veracity of their narratives? Would readers believe that they wrote their narratives themselves? Indeed, would they believe that their editors had played only a limited role in shaping what the texts conveyed? The formerly enslaved who could neither read nor write, who solely relied on editors to compose their narratives, would also have to wonder about the editor's role in addition to the questions faced by the authors writing for themselves. But, on top of that, they questioned whether the editors captured their stories accurately, whether they inserted any additional (unapproved) information, and whether they engaged in any other compromising activities in light of the author's inability to verify the written text. The reading public's interpretation of these "as-told-to" narratives must also consider these issues and still appreciate the insights these narratives of slavery can offer.

The example of Truth's speech is instructive because the debate about the authenticity of representation—for example, whether "Ain't I a Woman" or "Arn't I a Woman" or "I am a Woman" best captures Truth's word choices, tone, and delivery—reflects a larger conversation about the documentation, preservation, and interpretation of a literary or written culture that possesses oral roots, and one where an orality continues to develop alongside the written tradition. Considering Truth's speech and the questions it raises can open up a wider discussion of oral narratives of slavery that were recorded. These texts play an important role in telling the story of Black people's thinking about slavery, and they complement the separate tradition of narratives of slavery that the enslaved or formerly enslaved wrote for themselves.

Black oral traditions and the problems of the archive

Without a doubt, the earliest examples of Black thinking about slavery and firsthand accountings of slavery occurred orally as newly enslaved, recently kidnapped, and otherwise dispossessed Black people responded to the emerging and then persistent condition of enslavement. From the Middle Passage to the auction block, from the auction block to the plantation, from the plantation back to the auction block, and then to another plantation, from the beginnings to the present, Black people have actively engaged with the ideas, practices, and people that considered them chattel, commodifiable, or disposable. This claim does not presuppose that they all resisted or acquiesced. Rather, it acknowledges that, as human beings capable of experiencing a range of emotions, thoughts, and feelings, enslaved Black people—from their arrival—opined about their own statuses and the statuses of others. This interiority of Black life is what post–civil rights and cinematic turns to slavery explicitly try to capture as they use critical fabulation to create a representational archive that is otherwise absent. That body of cultural production and its related cultural criticism have in turn inspired scholarly examinations of Black interiority in traditional autobiographical narratives of slavery, and in narratives of slavery more broadly.

The historical record of course lacks documentation of the conversations Black people must have had among each other while working on the plantation or spending time with their kin. Written diaries in which they reveal their intimate thoughts, fears, aspirations, and longings also elude the public record. Yet Black people possessed all of these experiences, and to better grasp and reconstruct Black life during the nation's formation, scholars can also continue to examine "approximate narratives," narratives not necessarily produced or recorded by Black people but that nonetheless give insights (even if unintentionally so) into Black life and Black thinking. Approximate narratives emerge in a variety of contexts and forms, including legal records, literature, historical ledgers, poetry, newspaper articles, advertisements, pension bureau records, songs (and their performances), preaching, and so forth. By recording what Black people appear to have said or not said, done or not done, thought or not thought, felt or not felt, approximate narratives bring scholars close enough—in proximity—to important elements of Black life that they can then examine more critically and thoroughly.

By widening the lens to sources beyond self-written archives, we can gain a richer understanding of the who, what, where, when, and why of autobiographical narratives of slavery. This in turn provides us with a more comprehensive picture of the nuances of

Black experience, with thoughts about, and feelings toward, slavery and its afterlives. Turning to oral traditions in particular offers a broader historical frame for engaging narratives of slavery *before* and *after* Emancipation. A significant number of autobiographical narratives of slavery, for example, emerge between 1840 and 1865 during the height of the abolitionist movement. Yet oral narratives of slavery circulate long before the proliferation of written autobiographical narratives dominate the cultural scene, and persist long after legal slavery ends. They also represent a wider range of experiences, since those enslaved people who penned and published their own accounts were a self-selected, and in a sense more privileged, subclass of those who endured slavery. The oral tradition thus anchors the life and afterlives of slavery that the written tradition also takes up, and it adds another set of perspectives and epistemologies to their study.

Negro spirituals

In African American literary and cultural studies, spirituals (i.e., Negro spirituals) have played an integral role in the formation of a written African American literary tradition. By positioning spirituals at the tradition's beginnings, and by connecting the oral to the written, scholars have expanded the ways that people understand "literacy" and captured the continuity between prewritten texts and those that were written later. Besides literary scholars, scholars of Black religion and Black (liberation) theology also have found spirituals to be particularly helpful when examining Black people's reflections on God, freedom, and enslavement. As Black people increasingly encountered the Second Great Awakening, they learned and interpreted biblical ideas and stories on their own terms, rejecting some of the interpretations that their captors had tried to force upon them in the first generations of the institution. The spirituals evidence this thinking and have thus been of importance to a wide range of constituencies.

Some critics have argued that spirituals evidence Black complacency—reveal that enslaved Black people had merely acquiesced to slavery and had accepted their owners' instructions to "obey their master." This group would hold that the enslaved did not resist what pro-slavery uses of religion foisted upon them. Others, however, have insisted that the spirituals evidence Black creativity and ingenuity, as Black people used the spirituals to resist slavery at a time when society consistently called into question the very humanity of Black people and their abilities to do so. That humanity declared, too, that God had a plan for liberation for Black people and that the freedom would be *both* metaphorical and literal, spiritual and physical.

These two perspectives about spirituals hinge on the weight one ascribes to the so-called *otherworldliness* of the spirituals, or the belief that spirituals primarily (or only) focus on an afterlife—that they articulate a heavenly freedom but not an earthly one. Those who decry spirituals identify their perceived passivity: a focus on an afterlife dissipated the will of the enslaved to fight against slavery. Yet this interpretation fails to appreciate the conditions under which Black people would have expressed them and the creative ways that Black people in fact used them to resist enslavement. Put another way, enslaved Black people harnessed owners' beliefs that Black people's spirituals referred *only* to symbolic freedom in the afterlife as a way to resist and denounce slavery, and to, at times, plan and organize their escapes.

Old Testament and New Testament stories of liberation that highlight deliverance resonated in the Black imagination, and thus we find those stories often occurring in popular spirituals. From Moses's deliverance of the Israelites ("Go Down Moses"), to Daniel's deliverance from the Lion's Den ("Didn't My Lord Deliver Daniel"), to the general life and ministry of Jesus ("Steal Away to Jesus"), the spirituals reveal liberation as a central tie that binds them. That is, Black people *typologically identified* with these biblical examples and, in the process, imbued the spirituals with multiple meanings. A chant from "Steal Away to Jesus"—"that my Lord calls me by the thunder"—for example, often gets interpreted as also meaning that during a thunderstorm an enslaved person will make a move toward freedom. The Lord's call is the Lord providing rain so that the enslaved might escape and circumvent dogs' abilities to catch their scents or for owners to see them well in the stormy weather.

This both/and element of the spirituals demonstrates how enslaved Black people masked their meaning so that they could subvert, challenge, and/or undermine the status quo. Put another way, knowing they could not explicitly communicate their plans to escape or otherwise challenge slavery openly, enslaved Black people used Negro spirituals as one way to demonstrate their ability to, in the words of Ralph Ellison, "slip the yoke and change the joke." While to some it appeared they were only *acquiescing* to slavery, to others it was clear that they were all the while working against slavery. Negro spirituals thus also provide insights into how Black people understood Christianity in general, and used the strand of liberation they found running through it to make sense of their lives and political conditions during and after Emancipation.

Negro spirituals thus reveal how enslaved Black people coded their messages with multiple meanings as a way to undermine the institution of slavery. The concepts of masking and subversion are useful tools in interpreting the messages the songs communicated, and they help us to understand the multiple roles Negro spirituals played for enslaved Black people. *Masking* refers to the ways the songs relayed multiple meanings and communicated different messages to their multiple audiences. Masking makes room for the spirituals to remain otherworldly and worldly simultaneously. While the enslaved sang about a promised deliverance in the afterlife, they *also* sang to communicate their escape plans from their current enslavement. The success of their efforts hinged on their ability to outwit the owners who thought them incapable of communicating in ways imperceptible to owners, and their belief that slavery contradicted God's will toward freedom, which made them work diligently to free themselves from enslavement.

This body of cultural production points to yet another important way that Black people were engaging extant discourses about slavery and their own positions in society. The Negro spirituals set a foundation that subsequent Black freedom struggles would invoke as they fused or adapted spirituals, gospel, and the blues to articulate their freedom dreams and organize freedom movements. Negro spirituals thus provide insights into the ways that enslaved Black people made sense of the sociopolitical environment in which they found themselves and provided them with a vehicle to express their thoughts about slavery and challenge its underlying racial logics.

WPA narratives of slavery; the masses of Black people

During the Great Depression, the Works Progress Administration (WPA) embarked upon an ambitious project to interview formerly enslaved African Americans who could provide firsthand recollections of their experiences during slavery. By the mid-1930s, enslaved children born right before Emancipation would have been at least 70 years old, and their parents, who had endured slavery and possessed more expansive memories of enslavement, would have been, of course, a generation older. In some ways, the project to collect autobiographical accounts of slavery while this final or second-to-final generation was still alive gave the mission a sense of urgency. These interviews with the formerly enslaved do provide another resource for exploring the life and afterlives of slavery, as interviewers attempted to capture a glimpse of the experiences of the formerly enslaved during and, in some instances, after slavery.

The federal government funded the WPA interviews, but individual states played a key role in implementing the processes, as they hired and deployed interviewers into Black communities to conduct the interviews. While the Roosevelt administration had hoped to create a federal repository containing all of the transcribed oral histories, administrative and logical issues initially complicated this effort. Researchers, and anyone else who is curious, can now access written transcriptions and oral recordings of the original interviews. While the WPA narratives had been compiled by the early 1940s, interest in them grew in the 1970s, following the modern civil rights movement, when increased scholarly interest in slavery and its legacies responded to civil rights and Black Power demands to retell, and tell more accurately, this phase of American history.

WPA narratives expand the narratives of slavery archives to include ordinary citizens who had lived through slavery and were enduring its afterlives. They serve as the needed complement to the self-selected subset of narratives written by the formerly enslaved, like Douglass and Jacobs, revealing a wider range of social classes and experiences.

While important and rich sources, the WPA narratives and their representations of Black experiences raise concerns similar to those that emerged in critical discussions about Sojourner Truth's iconic speech. In other words, readers or listeners are left to wonder how differences in race, class, gender, sexuality, and literacy between interviewers and interviewees impact and mediate what emerges in the transcribed WPA narratives of slavery. That is, the written transcriptions relied solely upon the editorial decisions of the interviewers. By consenting to be interviewed, the formerly enslaved tacitly agreed to surrender their words, the representation of those words, and the depiction of their lives more broadly to the interviewer.

These facts, coupled with the expected yet vast discretion interviewers possessed over how to conduct the interviews—despite a plan to use a standardized set of interview questions—nonetheless yielded a complex set of narratives of slavery that give insights into the lives of the enslaved during and after slavery, the ways race and racial stereotypes inform the narratives and their framings, and how slavery's initial disenfranchisement of the enslaved reconfigures itself to keep Black people disempowered after slavery well into the first four decades of the twentieth century. WPA interviewers gathered these stories in the "Deep South," where the stratification that Jim Crow facilitated and exacerbated serves as an ever-present reminder of Black people's second-class citizenship. During the interviews, the subjects had this fact on their minds, and their contemporary surroundings and conditions connect with the stories of slavery that they related. In this sense, their accounts emerge to tell the history of slavery when its lived reality—its afterlife—is far from over.

When reading WPA narratives of slavery, protocols for reading, interpreting, understanding, and making use of oral yet recorded narratives of slavery can prove useful. The reader must remain cognizant of the racial identities of the interviewee (Black) and interviewer (usually white) and the related power differentials given to those racial differences. Readers must also bear in mind the specific questions the interviewer asks as well as any follow-up ones, how the interviewer and other editors edited the content, and how the interviewer's and other editors' overall framing of the interview shapes the information the narratives provide. These editorial processes lead Sharon Musher to conclude that WPA narratives could be "third-hand or even forth-hand accounts." These considerations also point to broader concerns about truth, voice, and authenticity and can raise understandable skepticism about what the formerly enslaved reportedly said. Yet these concerns do not diminish the usefulness of what the narratives can reveal. Rather, they provide a useful context for framing how to read them. They also point to the significance of narratives not written by Black people unfolding as valuable archives across time to access Black people's thoughts, perspectives, and feelings.

The volume *Alabama WPA Slave Narratives: From Interviews with Former Slaves* possesses a title page that includes an important subtitle—*A Folk History of Slavery in the United States*—that at once grants the importance of the experiences of ordinary enslaved African Americans—the folk—and that simultaneously attempts to curtail the degree to which the histories that these folk illuminate can function as *official* historiographies of slavery. Conducted between 1936 and 1938, the interviews contained in volume 1 are from people who lived in Alabama during this time, but who had not been necessarily enslaved in Alabama. On the one hand, this detail frustrates anyone who desires to use the narratives to understand geographical trends or experiences of the people interviewed. On the other hand, the nonspecificity of origins also points to a general and generic trend that exists for Black life post-Emancipation.

Although interviewers had the assignment of using a standard set of questions, the interviews themselves follow multiple formats. These differences reflect the magnanimity of the project and the difficulty of establishing a uniform practice across, or even within, states. An interview with Charity Anderson, for example, includes a prefatory description that provides her age and includes an assessment of her current physical condition. An interview with Tom Baker, by contrast, begins with a remark he makes about remembering slavery. An interview with Ank Bishop includes a photograph of Bishop standing in front of an open window on the side of his house. Yet an interview with Nelson Birdsong lacks any photographic evidence. An interview with Sally Murphy attempts to quote Murphy's speech and dialect but intersperses within it "standard English." But the interview of Siney Boner attributes to Boner a dialect that approaches that of Sojourner Truth in the "Arn't I a Woman" rendition of her famous speech.

This volume of the interviews lacks an editorial introduction that explains or contextualizes any of these issues. Readers therefore do not know for certain why and how some of these differences emerged. For example, should all of the interviews contain photographs of the interviewee? If so, what type of evidence did the photographs provide? Did they function as a form of an "authenticating document" for the interviews? Were some photographs taken but lost during the archival process? Do some exist but were never archived? Did any of the formerly enslaved decline being photographed? How do readers interpret their postures, gazes, and positioning in these "oral yet recorded" narrative photos? Do their gazes, for example, tell a story that might complicate or contradict what they have reportedly "told" an interviewer? Do the photos "speak" more candidly than their actual words because the formerly enslaved remain skeptical of how the interviews might have been used? These questions are worth considering, even if they can't be answered. They foreground how the Black people in the interview, and the formal elements of the interview, can work together to provide additional insights to the information that the formerly enslaved provide about the durability of slavery and Jim Crow.

An examination of WPA narratives of slavery thus also points to the ways that the historical context in which the interviews occurred (Jim Crow South during the Great Depression), as well as the historical context that the interviews reference (slavery), exist on a historical continuum. Inasmuch as the interviews elucidate details about Black life before Emancipation and Reconstruction, they also illuminate how slavery's aftermath reaches into the contemporary moment of the 1930s. Arguably, the interviews reveal an ongoing disenfranchisement, poverty, and second-class citizenship that echoes the experiences the formerly enslaved had had during slavery.

A host of common themes, for example, emerge throughout the interviews, and these similarities point to the competing purposes for which the narratives could be used. This collection of WPA narratives reinforces the ideas that the interviewees had "good owners," that the institution of slavery was not "*that* bad," and that they were "better off" in slavery than post-Emancipation. For example, Charity Ann recalls:

> I kin remember de days w'en I was one of de house servants . . . Us did'n' know nothin' but good times den . . . My ole Massa was a good man. He treated all his slave kind, and took good care of 'em. But, honey, all de white folks wan't good to dere slaves. . . . But, thank de Lawd, I had good white folks and dey sho' did trus' me, too.

Her "good times den" remark, when contrasted with her previous lamentation of her current poverty, does not suggest a longing for slavery per se. Rather, this tendency for the narratives to romanticize the institution of slavery may more so reflect the contemporary social and racial relations at the time of interview than it does a nostalgia for slavery or its related conditions. It might also reveal much about the interviewer's nostalgia. Needless to say, it speaks poorly of the Jim Crow era if it made someone reflect on their experience of slavery with any note of nostalgia whatsoever.

In the 1930s, uncertainty about the government's use of this information would have perhaps compelled the interviewee to respond cautiously, if at all. Dominant narratives of slavery at the time had continued to insist on slavery's mildness, emphasize the lack of agency of the enslaved, and underscore the beneficial effects slavery had for the enslaved and for society more generally. These trends would thus impact how the formerly enslaved responded to the questions as well as how the interviewers documented those responses. In important instances where the formerly enslaved compared the material conditions of slavery to their contemporary ones, they provided insights into an important fact: not that they were better off in slavery, but rather, post-Reconstruction, the afterlives of slavery replicated the racial hierarchies, economic subordination, and social antagonisms that slavery had structured, systematized, and perfected. Much of the ugliness of slavery had not been left behind. During the Great Depression, for example, in Black communities, Roosevelt's New Deal was known as the "raw deal," as the unemployment insurance excluded tenant farmers and domestic workers. As Black people were disproportionately represented in those lines of work, their inability to benefit from the social safety net made their economic prospects even more dire during this national depression.

Scholars who have reviewed a large swath of WPA narratives have emphasized the mistrust that existed between the Black residents and white government interviewers. This skepticism toward the interviewers' potential motives and subsequent uses might account for an underreporting of slavery's hardships from the formerly enslaved. Additionally, interviewees might also over-accentuate so-called fond memories of slavery. During slavery, owners would send spies to ask enslaved people about their living conditions and the treatment they received from their owners. Any actual or perceived complaint, as the *Narrative of the Life* and *Incidents in the Life* confirm, could result in punishment, sale, or death. The formerly enslaved people participating in these interviews would have had these old practices in mind, and these memories reasonably would have shaped their responses.

In Virginia, where the interviewers were Black, a different set of recollections emerges. In *Virginia Slave Narratives: A Folk History of Slavery in Virginia from Interviews with Former Slaves*, interviewees explicitly call attention to the violence and brutality of slavery, including the ways that owners raped enslaved Black women and how they resisted. In Susie Byrd's interview with Fannie Berry, for example, Berry explains the horrors that awaited Black women, how some fought back, and how others unfortunately could not stave off sexual violation as she had done. Berry elaborates:

> I wuz one slave dat de poor white man had his match. See Miss Sue? Dese here ol' white men said, "what I can't do by fair means I'll do by foul." One tried to throw me, but he couldn't. We tussseled an' knocked over chairs an' when I got a grip I scratched his face all to pieces; and dar wuz no more bothering Fannie from him; but oh. Honey, some slave would be beat up so, when dey resisted, an' sometimes if you'll 'belled de overseer would kill yo'. Us Colored women had to go through a plenty, I will tell you.

Berry's insights cast the threat of sexual violence as quotidian and white people's willingness to punish Black women's resistance as frequent. Yet she suggests that Black women resisted, even at the risk of death, and that Black resistance worked; after all, that particular man did not bother her again.

Berry's candor also emphasizes the importance of a Black interviewer establishing a rapport and comfort with the interviewee to get a more complete perspective of how the enslaved experienced slavery. For instance, Berry's replies demonstrate comfort and trust of Byrd. "See Miss Sue," for example, points to a moment where Berry will confide some intimate details. When she ends with "I will tell you," the "you" is specific. That is, she will tell Byrd these details about what Black women endured, but not necessarily another interviewer. These moments in the interviews have to be considered in this context because Virginia indeed was one of the few states that had employed a significant number of Black interviewers to complete the project. The perception of racial allegiance reasonably explains the seemingly more candid responses the formerly enslaved interviewees gave about these particularly grotesque aspects of abuse they and others experienced during slavery. They more willingly shared candidly their feelings, thoughts, analyses, and epistemologies because they did not believe the Black interviewers wanted to use the interviews to further disenfranchise them. To the contrary, they may have hoped that their candidness would improve their material conditions, depending on how the state or federal government used the information they provided.

WPA narratives of slavery, as oral yet recorded narratives, provide useful insights into how ordinary Black citizens who might never otherwise contribute to a book experienced slavery. Readers must contextualize and examine the conditions of production, reception, and distribution when reading, interpreting, and analyzing these as-told-to WPA narratives of slavery. They provide a way to hear the voices of Black people who had lived several decades beyond slavery's end and to see the historical similarities of Black life before and after Emancipation.

Black-produced oral yet recorded narratives of slavery

While significant, the recordings made by the WPA were not the first recorded as-told-to testimonies of formerly enslaved Black people. Decades before the WPA project, Black abolitionists had recorded the experiences that the formerly enslaved had endured. In 1872, for example, William Still published *The Underground Railroad Records: Narrating the Hardships, Hairbreadth Escapes, and Death Struggles of Slaves in Their Efforts for Freedom*. As a Black "conductor" on the Underground Railroad, Still was clearly an ally to formerly enslaved Black people. He continued his advocacy by making a concerted effort to create a written record for the formerly enslaved people he encountered.

However brief, the vignettes in *The Underground Railroad Records* give important details not only about the lives of the enslaved prior to their escapes, but also later as they continued their pursuits of freedom. Slavery follows them not only because, as a result of the Fugitive Slave Act of 1850, their freedom remains tenuous in the absence of formal Emancipation (the Emancipation Proclamation) and the abolition of slavery

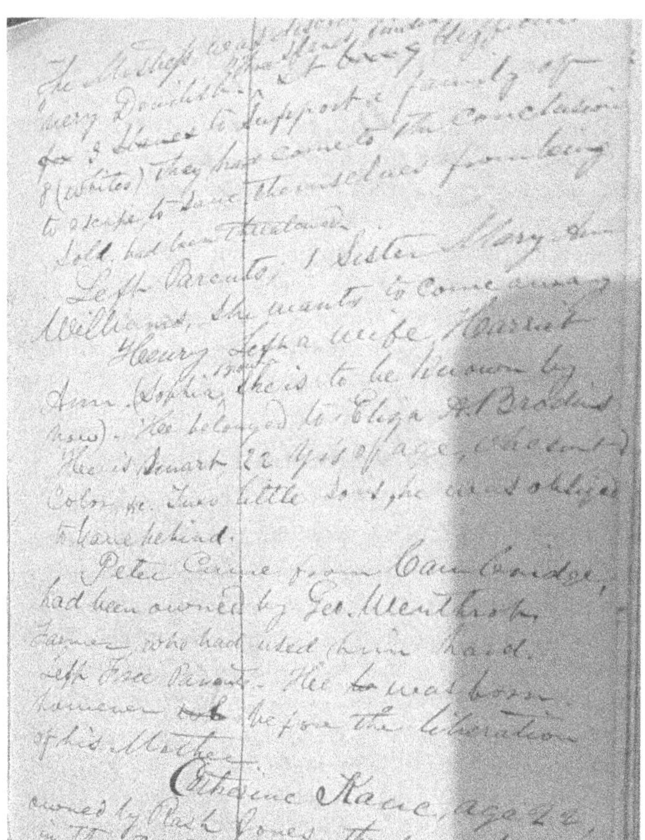

5. An example of the detailed notes that Black abolitionist William Still kept of the self-emancipated Black people he encountered on the Underground Railroad during his leadership in Pennsylvania. These notes helped him to then write *The Underground Railroad Records*.

(the Thirteenth Amendment), but also because they have family members that remain bound within slavery, or others who too have escaped, and with whom they want to reconnect. This desire to reunite with family informs the details the formerly enslaved provide to Still, how Still recounts the details, and subsequent requests for assistance that come alive in the text. In going on the record, the survivors of slavery call out for their loved ones.

Still's narrative thus brings together three interrelated voices to create narratives of slavery that show Black people's movement from slavery, to personal Emancipation or fugitivity, to a legalized freedom. Those are the voices of Still, the formerly enslaved people whose stories he tells, and voices of the advertisements that assist with potential family reunifications. Inasmuch as *The Underground Railroad Records* provides Still's narrative of the formerly enslaved people's experiences of enslavement, and of their self-expressed subsequent experiences post-self-emancipation, it also gives glimpses into the lives of the family members of the formerly enslaved, and all that they endured as part of the institution. Readers glean information about family members and their experiences during slavery based on what the formerly enslaved report. Importantly, there is also correspondence included in the book that demonstrates how Black abolitionists kept each other informed of the important work of securing Black people's freedom. For instance, Thomas Garrett wrote Still in 1860 to inform him that "Harriet Tubman is again in these parts. She arrived last evening from one of her trips of mercy to God's poor, bringing two men with her as far as New Castle. I agreed to pay a man last evening, to pilot them on their way to Chester County." This letter shows yet another way that narratives of slavery worked to abolish slavery and further the goal of Black enfranchisement. Still, Tubman, and Moss share a mutual goal, and Still's oral yet recorded narrative of slavery collects these efforts in one place to show the forcefulness and expansiveness of the network engaged in this work.

Whether it's the details that Still provides, the direct requests from the self-emancipated after they have left Philadelphia and correspond with Still, or the "family reunification" ads that Black people placed in newspapers after formal Emancipation, *The Underground Railroad Records* forcefully shows Black people engaging in a wide range of activities from their own vantage points to improve their lives during slavery's lives and afterlives. *The Underground Railroad Records* demonstrates the important relationships between the oral yet recorded and the self-written texts. Together, the two types of narratives contained in this singular publication create a Black archive of slavery—one that vividly depicts the lives and afterlives of slavery, and does so through Black voices and perspectives. Texts such as *The Underground Railroad Records* show the formative roles that Black abolitionists played in also preserving Black communities' narratives of slavery. In the process, a text such as this disrupts the primacy of (self-)written and autobiographical narratives of slavery. Moreover, it allows us to consider how oral, written, biographical, and extra-literary texts collectively create narratives of slavery that enhance the perspectives over which *traditional* autobiographical narratives of slavery have held extraordinary influence. All the while, it emphasizes the roles of Black people, Black voices, Black perspectives, and Black experiences in documenting slavery's reaches and effects.

Chapter 4
Slavery remade: Jim Crow narratives of slavery

Regardless of the uncertainties that post-Emancipation life would hold, Black people must have been elated following the demise of a brutal and inhumane system that had withheld citizenship rights and so much more from them. For both the formerly enslaved and so-called free Black people, the defeat of slavery signaled a potential turning point in American history that would provide unencumbered citizenship rights. The subsequent ratification of the Thirteenth, Fourteenth, and Fifteenth Amendments granted citizenship, guaranteed due process and equal protection under the law, codified the right to vote for Black men, and provided the legal and political bases on which they could build their hope. The passage of the Civil Rights Act of 1875 protecting their rights to enjoy public spaces and accommodations further propelled their optimism. In other words, they believed that the period of Reconstruction, the rebuilding of American society in the aftermath of the Civil War, would include them as citizens.

In the meantime, the Freedmen's Bureau, despite being underfunded and understaffed to execute its work effectively, had been facilitating their integration into society. By obtaining vital records (birth certificates), fighting for public education, obtaining paid labor, legally recognizing marriages, reuniting families, and establishing new mutual aid societies, Black people expressed a sincere desire to participate in American civic and political life. Contrary to pro-slavery arguments that had insisted that Black people would languish in the absence of the peculiar institution, Black people flourished and showed ambition. When they had access to opportunities, they, too, could succeed.

The government tried to protect Black people, to negotiate employment contracts, and to provide physical protection against white supremacist violence, yet these efforts lasted for approximately a decade. The end of Reconstruction, marked by the Tilden-Hayes Compromise following the 1876 election, put a dent in both Black political and economic advancement and the potential for further progress. While there certainly had been episodes of violence—material, physical, and ideological—against Black people during Reconstruction, the "official end" of federal efforts to economically, legally, and militarily support Reconstruction's ambitious aims simultaneously marked the beginning of white terror against Black people and Black communities. For each of the constitutional rights, for example, that the Thirteenth, Fourteenth, and Fifteenth Amendments conferred for Black people, laws emerged throughout the United States in the late nineteenth century that undermined those rights. These laws, known as Black Codes, essentially reinstituted slavery by curtailing and revoking the rights of Black people, conferring second-class citizenship upon them, reinforcing racial hierarchies that were central to slavery's enforcement, and eroding any economic and political progress that Black people had made since Emancipation. The so-called Redemptionists and other white supremacist sympathizers were hell-bent on thwarting Black progress and enacted a range of formal and informal policies, procedures, and customs to achieve their goals. The culmination of their efforts resulted in what the historian Rayford Logan would refer to as the nadir of race relations.

For every right the Thirteenth, Fourteenth, and Fifteenth Amendments conferred, white supremacists found implicit and explicit ways to curtail and/or outright deny it. For instance, the Thirteenth Amendment abolished slavery (except as penal punishment) and granted Black people citizenship rights, but the development of a penal system that targeted Black people and disproportionately arrested and sentenced them to hard labor ensured a steady source of free labor for states that used the exception clause to support convict leasing and earn revenue. The Fourteenth Amendment granted due process and equal protection under the law, but states such as Georgia and Tennessee actively supported vigilante violence by lynching accused Black people and denying them access to police protection or trials. The Fifteenth Amendment guaranteed Black men the right to vote, but literacy tests, poll taxes, and grandfather clauses arose to effectively deny Black men the right to participate in democracy.

These actions were intended to maintain the racial hierarchies that slavery had demanded, exploit Black labor, dilute Black political power, subordinate Black people and Black culture, and criminalize Black resistance. They were just some of the ways that the short-lived progress felt by Black people was cruelly reversed in this period. Black activists, writers, preachers, leaders, and ordinary citizens recognized these infringements and used a multitude of mechanisms to convey their displeasure with the ways that the post-Emancipation era was re-instituting slavery and creating slavery's afterlife. They called for the reconstruction of a fair and just society in which Black people could live and thrive.

While a series of state codes, laws, and practices had set the stage on which Black progress could be undone, the most damning blow occurred in 1896 when the Supreme Court rendered its ruling in the *Plessy v. Ferguson* case. Lauded by civil rights activists as a case that would affirm Black people's rights, the ultimate ruling did the opposite; here, the Supreme Court ruled that "separate but equal" public accommodations for Black people remained legal. Federalizing Jim Crow segregation, this ruling reinforced second-class citizenship for Black people, ensured that public accommodations remained separate, and insulated from any legal recourse the reality of unequal, inequitable, and subpar accommodations. That is, in practice, as long as there was an option for Black people, regardless of the *qualitative disparity* that existed between it and the one for "whites only," there did not exist a legal remedy to address its unequalness. The point and effect of the ruling were to re-enforce what the 1847 *Dred Scott v. Sandford* decision had stated plainly. Black people did not have any rights that white people were bound to respect, not even in light of Emancipation, the Thirteenth through Fifteenth Amendments, or the Civil Rights Acts. The *Plessy v. Ferguson* decision inaugurated the next chapter of the formalized, systematized, and legalized exclusion and seclusion of Black people that remained intact until the Supreme Court's ruling in the *Brown v. Board of Education* (1954) case overturned it and the Civil Rights Acts of the 1960s outlawed different types of discrimination.

The Black press, Black activists, Black clergy, Black politicians, and everyday Black citizens worked against the intensifying efforts to normalize the afterlives of slavery by creating more Black institutions to blunt their effects, by imploring the federal government to overturn them, and by encouraging citizens to resist them and assert their citizenship rights despite them. Late nineteenth- and early twentieth-century Black institution-making built on the foundations of exemplars such as John Russwurm and Samuel Cornish (*Freedom's Journal*), the African Methodist Episcopal Church (Wilberforce University), and the Free African Society (benevolent society). From the creation of Black Greek Letter Organizations (BGLOs), beginning in 1906; to civic organizations such as the National Association for the Advancement of Colored People (NAACP) in 1909, the National Association for Colored Women (NACW) in 1896, and the Universal Negro Improvement Association (UNIA) in 1919; to normal and industrial schools such as Lucy Laney's Haines

6. National Association for the Advancement of Colored People (NAACP) meeting in Chicago in 1917. Jane Addams, W. E. B. DuBois, Bishop Lee, and C. E. Bentley are among the Black leaders and citizens attending.

Normal and Industrial Institute in Georgia; to the writings, speeches, activism, and debates of Booker T. Washington, Ida B. Wells, W. E. B. Du Bois, and Anna Julia Cooper, Black people launched a multipronged campaign to fight for the citizenship rights that they deserved.

Writings (essays, fiction, poetry, nonfiction, and historiographies) and speeches (later transcribed and published) persisted as important mediums through which Black people swayed the public's opinions about their deservedness of citizenship rights. As the nation grew more hostile to Black people's participation in what Gene Jarrett describes as formal politics, or traditional modes of political engagement like voting, Black people's use of informal politics, or cultural production like speeches and op-eds, adopted an even greater importance. Their written records have produced a body of Jim Crow narratives of slavery that respond in particular to the sociopolitical circumstances affecting Black life in the wake of Reconstruction's official ending in 1877. Booker T. Washington's *Up from Slavery* and Ida B. Wells's *A Red Record*, both Jim Crow narratives of slavery, demonstrate the range of solutions that Black people proposed to fight against the political disenfranchisement and violence during Jim Crow that echoed the experiences Black people had endured during slavery. These texts, as examples of their genre, show how Black people actively advocated for their rights and serve to reinforce how slavery remains a central narrative even after Emancipation. They also show us why cultural production created during Jim Crow deserves analysis as narratives of slavery.

Booker T. Washington's "Atlanta Exposition" speech and *Up from Slavery*

Black people in general, and Black leaders in particular, shared the goal of improving Black people's economic, social, political, and educational standings and potential in the aftermath of Emancipation and Reconstruction. Yet they differed on the best and most constructive ways to achieve these goals. Recall that during slavery, gradualists and immediatists had agreed that slavery should end, but offered different timelines and processes to end it. Post-Emancipation, Black leaders and thinkers similarly proposed sometimes competing, sometimes conflicting, and sometimes congruent plans for Black people's advancement. Some leaders, for example, argued for a more reserved self-help approach that prioritized self-sufficiency, educational attainment, and property ownership, but did not explicitly demand political and civil rights. They also did not explicitly contest the very white supremacy that limited Black citizens' rights. Others believed Black people could and should help themselves, while still calling upon the federal government to protect and assist. They demanded immediate civil and political rights for Black people, and they specifically named white supremacy and anti-Black racism as threats to Black communities and democracy more generally.

This latter group believed that by not requesting civil and political rights immediately, Black communities would be foregoing the most critical protections necessary for any future successes. The debate between the two groups essentially questioned the degree to which the government should provide protections for Black people and their rights *and* facilitate Black people's long-term integration into the body politic. These debates had existed in Black communities since Emancipation, but in 1895 they leapt into the broader American political discourse on race relations; it was in that year that Booker T. Washington delivered his famed and perhaps infamous "Atlanta Exposition" speech, which critics also refer to as the "Atlanta Compromise" speech.

Born during slavery in 1856, author of *Up from Slavery: An Autobiography* (1901), graduate of the Hampton Normal and Agricultural Institute (1875), and principal of the Tuskegee Normal and Industrial Institute (1881), Booker Taliaferro Washington undoubtedly committed his life to advancing the economic, educational, and political rights of Black people. Although Washington publishes his autobiographical narrative of slavery, *Up from Slavery*, six years after he delivers the Exposition speech, it meticulously and methodically threads the ideas that figure prominently in the Exposition speech. As *Up from Slavery* evidences, Washington's investment in Black uplift remained deeply rooted in, and guided by, his beliefs that education should have a practical use that could be beneficial in the southern economy, that hard work and the demonstration of political readiness would allow Black people to become full citizens, and that *openly* or *publicly* calling attention to white supremacy would not improve Black people's economic or political lives.

Although some Black leaders may have disagreed with Washington's willingness to defer political and civil rights, Kevin Gaines clarifies that formerly enslaved people who sought economic self-sufficiency and property ownership found Washington's message appealing. While collective hopes for land redistribution would in fact require some type of governmental intervention, the appeal of economic stability and upward mobility likely resonated in their own rights. During Washington's tenure as Tuskegee's principal, he tested and developed the educational, economic, and political philosophies that he outlines in the Exposition speech. Washington insists that broader society can replicate the "Tuskegee model." As a postsecondary educational institution that specialized in vocational education, Tuskegee Institute prepared students in practical trades like carpentry, painting, dressmaking, and agriculture. Washington prided Tuskegee on training Black students to provide goods and services that benefited the broader (white) economy. Washington believed that this type of self-determination could make Black people indispensable to the (white) economy, and could encourage intra-racial business and collaboration that ultimately would result in Black people gaining their civil and political rights.

Washington expresses this point of view quite intensely in chapter 10 of *Up from Slavery* when he commends his plan for teaching students how to make bricks that they then use to literally build the Tuskegee campus, and to also enter business arrangements with the broader (white) community. As Washington recalls:

> The making of bricks taught me an important lesson in regard to the relations of the two races in the South. Many white people who had had no contact with the school, and perhaps no sympathy with it, came to us to buy bricks because they found out that ours were good bricks. . . . [T]he education of the Negro was not making him worthless, but that in educating our students we were adding something to the wealth and comfort of the community. . . . [O]ur business interests became intermingled. . . . This, in large measure, helped to lay the foundation for the pleasant relations that have continued to exist between us and the white people in that section, and which now extend throughout the South.

This passage, like several in *Up from Slavery*, romanticizes race relations between Black and white people in the South after slavery, and simultaneously stitches the onus of Black integration in American society to Black people's behavior.

This logic presupposes that Black people must prove their "worth" in order to *earn* their citizenship rights. Although white people enjoy citizenship rights without these extraordinary encumbrances, Washington publicly suggests that Black people should wait and earn theirs, less they prove themselves underprepared to handle citizenship's responsibilities or rattle white supremacy's feathers. Washington, like his contemporaries, presupposed that by emphasizing self-sufficiency and moral uprightness, Black people would prove their deservedness and counter negative stereotypes often used to justify white supremacy's explanations of its exclusion of or violence against Black people. Essentially, Black people were developing strategies to respond to the reality that slavery's most harmful ideas about Black people, Black intelligence, Black culture, and Black sexuality persist following Emancipation and, more perniciously, often emerge to continue their disenfranchisement. While self-help appealed to Black people and provided a way to circumvent white supremacy's attempts to completely constrict their abilities to succeed or improve, self-help strategies and philosophies did (and do) not always address the institutional and systemic dimensions of Black inequality in the aftermath of slavery's abolishment.

Essentially, Washington suggests, or at least his critics generally agree that he does, that Black people can out-behave white supremacy and that white people will see Black economic success as mutually beneficial. The race riots of 1898 in Wilmington, North Carolina, those of 1906 in Atlanta, Georgia, and those of 1921 in Tulsa, Oklahoma, would put additional pressure on Washington's idealized vision of economic mutuality improving race relations; Black economic (and political) success in these places arguably fueled the race riots, as white vigilantes and everyday citizens targeted Black businesses in particular in their efforts to destroy Black wealth and progress. Given the legal and extralegal ways that white supremacy attempted to curtail Black progress, debates remain about whether Washington was acquiescing to the status quo to avoid what Carol Anderson defines as white rage, or whether he was masking acquiescence as a way for Black people to circumvent the system and therefore subvert it in the process. Even if Black people could not possess all they deserved, according to Washington, they could have something. Either way, Washington finds himself in the afterlife of slavery, responding to labor, education, political, and economic conditions that, while not called slavery, mirror the conditions of enslavement and extend the life of slavery.

For Washington's promotion of self-determination, political acquiescence, and industrial education, he has earned the label of an *accommodationist*, which describes someone who accepts the sociopolitical order of the day, even if it requires embracing a subservient or inferior role. When Washington gave the speech in 1895, the effects of what the *Plessy v. Ferguson* Supreme Court decision (1896) would cement had begun to reverberate already. That is, individual states had already been implementing segregation policies even though the Supreme Court had yet to sanction "separate but equal" as legally acceptable. Black people were actively fighting to counter the extension of slavery vis-à-vis second-class citizenship. To their dismay, they believed Washington had accepted what would become the separate and unequal practices that the ruling facilitated, and that he had espoused second-class citizenship as a viable and necessary pathway for Black people to gain their full citizenship rights. Seemingly accepting segregation, Washington declares: "In all things that are purely social we can be separate as the fingers, yet one as the hand in all things essential to mutual progress."

For Washington, one can have "purely social" divisions and still maintain mutual progress. But separate and unequal facilities, access, and accommodations troubled this argument. While two separate spheres exist, unequal ones for Black people prohibit them from shaking the yoke of slavery. To the contrary, both separation and segregation were intended to reinforce slavery's organizing logics and ideologies vis-à-vis spatial difference. Washington concedes Black people's positioning in these spatial logics, reminding his listeners that "it is at the bottom of life we must begin and not at the top," and he underscores the point by noting that "the wisest among my race understand that agitation of questions of social equality is the extremest folly." Washington suggests he accepts segregation and the deferral of civil/political rights because Black people must work their way up from slavery, as the title of his autobiographical narrative of slavery makes clear. Admittedly, Washington also might have recognized the intractability of white supremacy and moved to insulate Black people from it.

Critics also suggest that Washington also overestimates the collective will white people will have toward eventual integration when he notes that "[i]f anywhere there are efforts to curtail the fullest growth of the Negro, let these efforts be turned into stimulating, encouraging, and making him the most useful and intelligent citizen." During the 1890s, the lynching of Black people had increased exponentially, which is why Ida B. Wells takes this subject up so forcefully in *A Red Record*. Washington's suggestion that white people who did not support Black progress might redirect their violence to efforts that would make Black people better—that is, "the most useful and intelligent citizen"—does not account for this particular reality. It also again emphasizes the need to fix Black behaviors as a way to cure white supremacy's depravations of Black citizenship rights. By 1895, there exists little question that "there are efforts to curtail the fullest growth of the Negro," because the terror against Black people is ubiquitous, and has, as Ida B. Wells had reported, caused exoduses of Black people from Atlanta, Texas, and Memphis to the "West." And finally, the idea "that no race that has anything to contribute to the markets of the world is long in any degree ostracized" might be turning a blind eye, for example, to how the skills, talents, and professions that Black people had exhibited since slavery continued to get economically exploited during and after Reconstruction—through sharecropping and then subsequent laws that criminalized changing or leaving a (white) employer without permission. These facts of Black life caution against Washington's optimism of the market and contributions to it changing the conditions of Black labor and the potential for economic success in the absence of pushback against white supremacy's aggression.

All of these examples in Washington's speech, as well as those that he elaborates upon in *Up from Slavery*, undermine the idea that a structured, systemic white supremacy akin to slavery—though referred to by different names—adversely affected Black life and progress. Washington essentially publicly rejects or at least questions the premise of slavery's afterlife. He instead offers an argument for slow progress that, however frustrating, remains necessary. Undoubtedly, this argument had its detractors, with W. E. B. Du Bois serving as a chief critic who calls attention to the contradictions and problems he sees in the ideas "Of Mr. Booker T. Washington and Others," which is the title of chapter 3 in *The Souls of Black Folk* (1903). In short, Du Bois argues that Washington's plan creates a triple paradox in that he promotes dignity, yet accepts a subservient position; promotes industrial education only, yet needs teachers trained in a liberal arts education to run his school; and promotes property ownership, but does not offer any legal way to protect that property in the absence of political or civil rights. Du Bois's frustration speaks to the competing visions Black leaders, activists, and ordinary citizens had about how to address the urgent reality of Black people's persistent inequality and oppression after Emancipation.

The perception that Washington was acquiescing to notions of Black inferiority and deferring the attainment of civil and political rights indefinitely, however, might be undermined by the actions that Washington took privately. His private actions not only acknowledged the persistence of white supremacy, but he also aided individuals and institutions in fighting to dismantle white supremacy and help Black people to achieve civil rights. Washington's personal papers, for example, as Jarvis Givens explains, revealed he had participated in several lawsuits that aimed to secure Black people their constitutionally guaranteed civil rights. This record shows that Washington used his capital to effectually fight against the systemic ways that states attempted to erode the Fourteenth Amendment (segregated train cars) and Fifteenth Amendment (grandfather clauses), as well as to keep Black people economically subordinated through sharecropping (debt peonage). This addition to the historical record allows one to argue that a savvy Washington grasped the political climate of the day and masked his acquiescence as an accomodationist in order to raise money for Tuskegee, train Black people in higher education, and undermine the white supremacy that limited Black people to industrial education in the first place. He clearly also used his own wealth to privately support Black causes that his antagonists wished he had publicly espoused.

Black people recognized education's presumed important role in advancing Black life, even when they offered different perspectives on how to approach the mission of educating Black people and re-educating the broader public—Black and white alike—who had been miseducated about the Negro. In fact, Anna Julia Cooper and W. E. B. Du Bois would later recognize the urgency of writing against dominant post-Emancipation and late/post-Reconstruction histories that insisted the abolition of slavery was an error because Black people had shown their inabilities to integrate into and function in society. Du Bois's *Black Reconstruction in America: An Essay toward a History of the Part*

Which Black Folk Played in the Attempt to Reconstruct Democracy in America, 1860–1880 (1935) rejected the trend among white historians' historiographies to mischaracterize Reconstruction's failures as proof of Black people's deficiencies and further evidence for the need for white paternalism or white supremacy. As late as the fourth decade of the twentieth century, Black people were still consciously responding to the hovering legacies of slavery that haunted Black life. That Du Bois publishes this book during the same period that the WPA was interviewing formerly enslaved Black people further reminds us of the multiple constituencies that were invested in expanding narratives of slavery to better understand its enduring legacies.

Ida B. Wells's anti-lynching crusade and *A Red Record*

Inasmuch as Black leaders, activists, thinkers, writers, and ordinary Black people stayed concerned about the educational, economic, and political rights for Black people during and after Reconstruction, Black people also remained preoccupied with the fact that Black civil rights were becoming increasingly elided in federal and state laws and undermined through federal and state judiciary rulings and decisions. In many ways, the facts of Black life and experience had further supported Du Bois's chief criticism against Washington's accommodationist plan—without political rights and the legal protections they afford, economic and educational attainments remained precarious because the capriciousness of white supremacy and anti-Black racism always threatened to upend any progress. The double-sidedness of the law complicated Black people's paths toward progress and citizenship rights. On the one hand, the Fourteenth Amendment promised equal protection and due process. On the other, local laws and customs also implicitly and explicitly made exceptions for unequal protection and no processes; increasingly and with impunity, white supremacist organizations such as the Klu Klux Klan, as well as ordinary white citizens and law enforcement agencies, terrorized (and allowed for the terrorizing) of Black people.

These extrajudicial and, in some cases, judicially sanctioned killings of Black people, through lynching or otherwise, lead anti-lynching crusader Ida B. Wells to encourage Black people to prepare for white vigilante violence by arming themselves. In the tradition of earlier activists such as Martin Delany and Henry Highland Garnet, Wells does not condone offensive attacks on white people yet insists that if attacked, Black people should respond in turn. Wells advises that "a Winchester rifle should have a place of honor in every Black home, and it should be used for that protection which the law refuses to give." Wells herself first purchased a pistol for self-protection after a white mob extracted her friend Thomas Moss from jail and then shot him because he had defended himself against a lawless attack on his successful Black business. Wells then obtains a gun, as she relates in *Crusade*, "because [she] expected some cowardly retaliation from the lynchers," "had already determined to sell [her] life as dearly as possible if attacked," and "felt if [she] could take one lyncher with [her], this would even up the score a little bit." Wells's subsequent anti-lynching crusade then foregrounds the rights of Black people to bear arms and defend themselves, especially in the absence of state and federal protections against violence. In making these claims, Wells simultaneously implores the federal government to uphold the Fourteenth Amendment for both Black people who abide by the law and even those who break it; neither ordinary law-abiding citizens nor ones who violate the law should be subjected to vigilante violence, and her Jim Crow narrative of slavery, *A Red Record: Lynching Tabulated Statistics and Alleged Causes of Lynching in the United States, 1892-1893-1894*, explicitly argues this point.

While Wells became an anti-lynching crusader from 1892 onward, she had had firsthand experience with how the logics of slavery continued to shape Black people's lives in society more generally,

7. Anti-lynching crusader Ida Barnett Wells, author of *A Red Record* and *Southern Horrors*, was part of a broader effort by Black people to build new institutions within their communities to provide for themselves as Black civil, Black cultural, and Black political rights continued to be eroded.

and the legal system in particular. Before the US Supreme Court ruled against Plessy in the mid-1890s, the Tennessee Supreme Court had ruled against Ida (Barnett) Wells. It reversed a lower court's decision ruling in Barnett's favor against the Chesapeake, Ohio, and Southwestern Railroad Company after a conductor had forcibly removed her from a *ladies'* railroad car. Whereas Ferguson's case drew attention to the racial discrimination against Black people in public accommodations more generally, Barnett's lawsuit particularized the gendered dimensions of the discrimination against Black women. Whether the image of the overly sexualized *Jezebel* or that of the domestic servant *mammy*, whatever Black women were, *ladies* they were not, according to slavery and post-slavery ideas about white womanhood. These, to use Patricia Hills Collins's phrase, "controlling images" of Black women played out during and after slavery; *lady* became a decidedly racialized term reserved primarily, if not solely, for white women. By attempting to travel in a ladies' car, and maintaining her rightful position to remain when commanded to exit,

Wells rejected the sociopolitical implications of the prevailing idea that Black ladies did not exist.

Recalling the event in *Crusade*, Wells shares:

> He tried to drag me out of the seat, but the moment he caught hold of my arm I fastened my teeth in the back of his hand. I had braced my feet against the back of the seat in front and was holding to the back and as he had already been badly bitten he didn't try it again by himself. He went forward and got the baggage man and another man to help him and of course they succeeded in dragging me out. They were encouraged to do this by the attitude of the white ladies and gentlemen in the car; some of them even stood on the seats so that they could get a good view and continued applauding the conductor for his brave stand.

Wells's recollection shows white men and white women bonding as they applaud the conductor and his assistants to forcibly remove Wells. But Wells makes a more striking point, one that presages Black people's experiences after Emancipation: law and public opinion would collude to mutually reinforce the idea that Black people shall forever remain second-class citizens. The reality of a civically and politically engaged Black citizenry enraged white supremacists as they sought legal and extralegal ways to all but re-enslave Black people.

At the heart of Wells's case lay the continued uneasiness of a post-Emancipation Black population in the white imagination and in presumable white-only spaces. That the white men and women "applauded" the conductors' dragging Wells out of the train car, rather than the fastening of her teeth to his arm, added to Wells's eventual desire to contest the white violence that killed Moss. But in the intervening decade, Wells's criticisms of Black misfortune in society had focused instead on Black communities and their behaviors. Wells's journalism did at times place some of the onus of Black progress on Black people's behavior. Unlike

Washington, however, Wells did leave a public record that clarifies her belief that ultimately systemic and institutional racism must be addressed in order for Black people to enjoy their citizenship rights.

Increased lynchings and governmental indifference toward them created an important cause that Black activists like Wells worked diligently to expose, contest, and criminalize in the post-Reconstruction era. Wells revealed the underreporting of lynchings in mainstream publications to show its pervasiveness and to challenge the notion that lynching was a one-off practice that random vigilantes enacted. She contested the idea that white men lynched Black men in order to avenge white womanhood to instead show that lynching starkly admonished Black people about the dangers of Black progress. She pushed for federal legislation to outlaw lynching by making it a crime. In *A Red Record*, Wells dispels common justifications for lynching and implores readers to become anti-lynching crusaders.

If one justification for lynching was that it avenged the honor of white women whom Black men allegedly had raped or otherwise sexually defiled, Wells unsettles this argument by calling forth the consensual sexual liaisons between white women and Black men, historicizing the false accusations of rape against Black men to excuse white violence against them, and demonstrating the arbitrariness of lynch law. Pro-slavery advocates had circulated the image and idea of the buck or brute to support their claims slavery was necessary to control Black people in general, and Black men in particular. This hypersexualized representation of Black men characterized them as threats to both white womanhood and society more generally. This notion of the Black man as a threat to white womanhood and society animated representations of Black men, and those representations reinforced the political climate that promoted white lawlessness against Black people. If the pre-Emancipation circulation of this image buttressed the idea that slavery had controlled and subdued the effects of the so-called Black bucks or brutes, the post-Emancipation spread of the idea aimed to reveal the failures of Reconstruction to contain such allegedly dangerous men.

In *A Red Record*, Wells argues that neither qualitative nor quantitative evidence supports the popular assertion that white men primarily lynch Black men to punish Black men for raping white women. Wells observes that the number of lynchings performed far exceeds the number of instances where rape was alleged, let alone committed. This image of Black men as rapists, however, often still justified lynchings. To support this claim, Wells notes that there are instances where Black men and white women have consensual sexual relationships. However, given the illegality of interracial consensual relationships, when the previously undisclosed relationships became public, white women alleged rape or white men assumed rape as the only possible way for such a liaison to occur. As Wells contextualizes, white men remained particularly invested in the narratives of rape, and, as the larger work points out, this obsession with Black men–white women rape might stem from the fact that, historically, white men's rape of Black women had gone unprosecuted. To elaborate, Wells offers the following:

> With the Southern white man, any mesalliance existing between a white woman and a colored man is a sufficient foundation for the charge of rape. The Southern white man says that it is impossible for a voluntary alliance to exist between a white woman and a colored man and therefore, the fact of an alliance is a proof of force. In numerous instances where colored men have been lynched on the charge of rape, it was positively known at the time of lynching, and indisputably proven after the victim's death, that the relationship sustained between the man and woman was voluntary and clandestine, and that in no court of law could even the charge of assault have been successfully maintained.

Wells rejects the Black man as rapist explanation for lynching, and the data she uncovered in her own research further disputes rape as the true reason for which white men lynch Black men. Elsewhere she adds that even if a Black man had raped a (white) woman, under the Fourteenth Amendment he would still be entitled to due process, including a fair trial, and not lynch law.

Wells's *A Red Record* thus anticipates Du Bois's insistence that the need for more narratives that speak against misinformation about Black people following Reconstruction would be necessary to undermine the ways that slavery's legacies continued to shape the popular and political imaginations.

Wells shows that lynching served as a mode of terror against Black people, warning them to, in Koritha Mitchell's phrase, "know their place" as it related to economic opportunities, sexual liaisons, educational possibilities, and any other mode of living to which white people thought themselves only or the most entitled. Indeed, the image of the Black man as rapist circulated to buttress lynching, to warn Black people against making progress and achieving, and to deny Black people their citizenship rights. But, in reality, as Wells argues throughout the book, and so eloquently puts it in the title of chapter 5 of *A Red Record*, Black people often were "lynched for anything or for nothing."

Wells, not just in her book but in her newspaper as well, wrote fervently to expose the false premises upon which lynching relied, and gave readers specific methods to use to challenge lynching's persistence in American life. In addition to imploring readers to circulate the knowledge contained in *A Red Record*, Wells encourages readers to wield economic power to boycott places that lynch, to use cultural and moral power in civic and religious organizations to pass resolutions to condemn lynching, to exercise political power to support the formation of a federal commission to investigate lynching, and to purchase and distribute her book in order to increase knowledge about lynching. Wells's journalism thus becomes an important tool in re-representing how people view and understand lynching, reframing conversations about the relationship between lynching and race, and calling for legislation that outlaws lynching and the slavery-based racial hierarchies that the practice was intended to solidify in the post-Emancipation era. Notably, federal anti-lynching legislation did not become a law until March 29, 2022.

Wells's *A Red Record* insists that, as Du Bois would echo later on, there was an urgent need for more narratives countering misinformation about Black people following Reconstruction. Such narratives could be powerful tools to help undermine the ways that slavery's legacies continued to shape the popular and political imaginations. In the era immediately following Emancipation and Reconstruction, Black activists, writers, thinkers, and ordinary citizens produced narratives that demonstrated how slavery and its legacies continued to circulate in American society. Although they did so in different ways, these Jim Crow narratives of slavery all demonstrated how slavery's reach continued to shape Black people's lives. They also demonstrated how Black people could offer differing perspectives as to how Black people should respond to various aspects of slavery's afterlife, from the legal to the extralegal, the social, and the economic. In the 1890s, the legacies of slavery were incorporated into Jim Crow practices; accordingly, future responses to the legacies of slavery would have to grapple with the legacies of Jim Crow as well.

Chapter 5
Freedoms on their minds: Post-civil rights narratives of slavery

When PBS adapted Ernest Gaines's novel *The Autography of Miss Jane Pittman* (1971) into a television movie (1974), it brought a multidimensional conversation about slavery and its legacies into the living rooms of everyday citizens. By the time the television series that adapted Alex Haley's *Roots: The Saga of an American Family* (1976) aired in 1977, an expansive set of literary and visual narratives of slavery had begun to permeate the cultural landscape. The civil rights, Black Power, and Black feminist movements had played important roles in (re)invigorating a renaissance in Black narratives of slavery in the post–civil rights era. From historical analyses, to fictive imagining, to poetic musings, to cinematic portrayals, Black artists, scholars, activists, and ordinary citizens alike desired a re-examination of slavery, its legacies, and how both had been represented and portrayed. In earnest, Black people demanded new, better, more accurate, and more comprehensive narratives of slavery that focused on Black people's perspectives, epistemologies, and accounts. From many vantage points, the ironically named "master" narratives of slavery—those produced by the so-called majorities—had failed to convey the complexity of Black agency, resistance, family life, diasporic retentions, kinship bonds, emotional interiority, and future aspirations. Black-produced narratives of slavery could correct these historical and artistic omissions, oversights, or mischaracterizations. But, more than a reactive posture, these narratives reveal the ingenuity of their producers as they foreground the ways that Black people transformed and continue to transform the world.

Gaines's novel, which is not an autobiography, follows the life of the protagonist, Miss Jane Pittman, whose lifetime spans from slavery until the modern civil rights movement. Miss Jane, who famed actress Cicely Tyson played in the television movie, participates in and witnesses the achievements and setbacks that typify Black people's quests for equality and civil rights from slavery through the 1960s (and present). Having lived for more than a century, the 110-year-old Miss Jane has survived slavery, Reconstruction, Jim Crow segregation, two world wars, and the Great Depression. Throughout each historical era, Miss Jane and the other Black people with whom she finds herself in community essentially attribute their current economic, political, social, and educational misfortunes to slavery and its legacies. New iterations of slavery remain in constant view for reading or television audiences. For instance, as a sharecropper, Miss Jane endures the threat of eviction and unemployment if she chooses to participate in or lead a civil rights demonstration during the 1960s.

That she remains a sharecropper approximately a century after legal Emancipation emphasizes again the points that sharecropping extends the economic exploitation of slavery and that Emancipation—the quest for Black freedom and full citizenship rights—persists as an ongoing struggle. Readers and viewers can interpret the threats that Miss Jane's employer makes to her as an interconnected web of dominance that aims to maintain white supremacy, curtail Black people's resistance, and extend the terrorism of slavery that Reconstruction had reinvented and that Jim Crow had legalized. By connecting seemingly distant historical events to current sociopolitical circumstances, the book and television movie help audiences to understand the sometimes indirect and other times direct ways the past and present shape each other. In making this point,

Gaines, as do other Black artists and cultural producers, contests the notions that American race relations progress linearly, that quests for civil rights end after the legislative victories that emerge in the 1960s, and that Black people's current and future demands for civil rights are disconnected from slavery and its legacies. *The Autobiography of Miss Jane Pittman* is a pivotal post–civil rights narrative of slavery, despite the fact that scholarly examinations of the text do not classify it as a contemporary re(imagining) of slavery. The title itself, which intentionally mis-signals the genre, usefully turns attention to the ways that post–civil rights narratives of slavery draw on a variety of sources, including the historical, fictive, imaginative, and (auto)biographical, to (re)present chattel slavery. Fictional depictions became powerful tools for doing so.

Without a doubt, the civil rights movement had increased Black people's employment, educational, and housing options, and ushered in a wave of Black elected officials in local, state, and federal offices. The Civil Rights Act of 1964, the Voting Rights Act of 1965, and the Fair Housing Act of 1968 share the responsibility for increasing Black people's access into spaces from which Jim Crow segregation had previously excluded them. But the 1970s witnessed an anti–civil rights backlash following the election of President Richard Nixon, and the social movements of the 1960s began to lose public support. The idea that the civil rights movement had corrected contemporary *and* past injustices became increasingly more popular. Within this logic, the legacies of Jim Crow and slavery either no longer mattered or were overstated. As national politics turned away from slavery and civil rights, a cadre of Black artists returned to the historical era of slavery to consider how that epoch returns to the present. They were concerned not only with the material and ideological relationships that existed; they also wanted to probe the psychological dimensions of slavery—how it had impacted and affected Black psyches.

As historians turned to historical documents and archives to uncover hidden, missing, excluded, or otherwise marginalized perspectives of the enslaved—including the WPA narratives of slavery—Black writers too found themselves compelled by the broader cultural imperative to rewrite or otherwise construct new narratives of slavery in the aftermath of the freedom struggles of the 1960s. These fictive returns to slavery, which often took the genre of the autobiographical narratives of slavery as their points of departure, situated enslaved Black people as the main subjects of the texts, and their experiences, perspectives, feelings, thoughts, and epistemologies as essential to understanding slavery *and* its aftermath. Indeed, these texts filled historical gaps that dominant narratives contained using critical fabulation and also rewrote intentional misrepresentations of Black resistance and agency. Black writers had taken exception, for example, to William Styron's novel *Confessions of Nat Turner*, and critics believed that Styron's portrayal of the enslaved emblematized the incorrect, racist, and otherwise problematic representations of slavery that dominant narratives portrayed.

Collectively, Black writers and cultural producers generated narratives of slavery that specifically placed Black people, Black perspectives, and Black experiences at the center of their storylines. Traditionally, these written works have been referred to as *neo-slave narratives*—fictional works that emulate first-person antebellum slave narratives. This volume, however, refers to them as *post-civil rights narratives of slavery* to emphasize how the aftermath of the modern civil rights movement serves as an impetus to think about slavery and/or Jim Crow (and legacies) in the texts. They share an abiding concern for trying to understand the interrelationship between the past and present and its influence on Black psyches.

Post-civil rights narratives of slavery: Past, present, and future times

Post-civil rights narratives of slavery use a variety of literary devices, rhetorical strategies, and historical events and incidents to articulate these connections. While a robust scholarly archive details the formal characteristics of post–civil rights narratives of slavery, most relevant to the discussion here is their role as post–civil rights era reimaginings of slavery. The post on this descriptor serves two functions. First, it turns attention to how after the legislative achievements of the modern civil rights movement a call for more texts produced by Black people to engage slavery emerged, and how these narratives responded with more nuanced perspectives. Second, it questions the degree to which the era is "after" civil rights, in the ways that the term "post" typically can signal, because Black people continue to live in the "long Emancipation," and the fight for civil rights and reparations continues as well.

In this context, "post" also questions, as do the narratives, what it means to be post-Emancipation when the logics and practices of slavery persist. This look to the past, present, and future to examine what the contours of freedom look like beyond legal freedoms explains why Angelyn Mitchell prefers the phrase "liberatory narrative" to neo-slave narrative; these narratives are as concerned, if not more, with articulating the many dimensions of freedom beyond legal Emancipation (historical) and legal civil rights (contemporary). Because of their focus on freedom, Mitchell thus calls these liberatory narratives and explains that they "provide new models of liberation by problematizing the concept of freedom" and are "primarily concerned with the nature of freedom." The persistence of racism and disenfranchisement after the obtainment of *legal* rights makes this task to redefine *freedom* even more urgent.

If the abolishment of slavery inaugurated a conversation about the legacies of slavery, the abolishment of legal segregation generated debates about the legacies of Jim Crow. While post–civil rights narratives of slavery develop their plots in a range of historical periods, from the antebellum period (Toni Morrison's *Beloved*) to the contemporary period of publication (Gayl Jones's *Corregidora*), the legacies of slavery and the legacies of Jim Crow provide two interpretive and contextualizing frameworks through which to analyze the texts. Memories often blur distinctions between time periods, and the texts use memories as mechanisms to examine *how* and *why* memories of the enslaved past intrude upon and matter in the present.

Post–civil rights narratives of slavery take up a wide range of focal points in order to explore slavery and its legacies and impacts. While imaginative, these narratives often find themselves revising or revisiting an earlier literary, historical, or cultural event in order to think about it and imagine it more fully. The authors' desire to rewrite, and thus make right, a previous representation of slavery and its legacies ties together the wide body of post–civil rights narratives of slavery.

Similar to how the abolitionist circuit used autobiographical narratives of slavery to sway abolitionist efforts, post–civil rights narratives of slavery too can be used to sway contemporary efforts for Black civil, cultural, and political rights. The underlying premise is that the mainstream archives of texts do not adequately portray the complexity of slavery and its legacies, nor do they prioritize Black people's insights and perspectives. Narratives of slavery written after the civil rights era not only fill in those gaps but also provide new conceptual frameworks to understand slavery. After Margaret Walker's *Jubilee* (1966), a representative listing of these texts includes Gayl Jones's *Corregidora* (1975), Ishmael Reed's *A Flight to Canada* (1976), Octavia Butler's *Kindred* (1979), David Bradley's *The Chaneysville Incident* (1981), Shirley Anne Williams's *Dessa Rose* (1986), Toni Morrison's *Beloved* (1987), Charles Johnson's *Middle Passage* (1990), J. California Cooper's *Family* (1991), Lorene Cary's *The Price of a Child* (1995), Edward P. Jones's *The Known World* (2003), Toni Morrison's *A Mercy* (2008), and Colson Whitehead's *The Underground Railroad* (2016).

We can consider Jones's *Corregidora* as one example text that explains the key themes and debates that Black writers exploring the legacies of slavery and Jim Crow have examined in the twentieth and twenty-first centuries. Through texts such as this, readers can juxtapose the end of slavery and Jim Crow with the persistence of both of their legacies to understand how Black writers think about and imagine freedom beyond the legal ends of these eras and practices. The narratives explore, for example, what it would take—materially and psychologically—for slavery to be more fully understood. Narratives like *Corregidora* can lay bare for readers the interiority of Black people—their thoughts and feelings—allowing readers to consider how slavery and its aftermath have *material* and *psychological* impacts. Such post–civil rights narratives of slavery break through to readers in powerful ways and force them to respond to the adverse legacies of slavery and Jim Crow.

A renaissance of post–civil rights narratives of slavery from Black cultural producers

Post–civil rights narratives of slavery turned a sharper eye toward the processes that more generally construct narratives, including historical ones. The proliferation of post–civil rights narratives of slavery, and the literary and cultural criticism that they generated, enhanced conversations about the ways, for example, that histories of slavery were not mere recollections of facts and events. Rather, there were processes and choices, often deliberate ones, that led to the overrepresentation of so-called master narratives of slavery that diminished Black people's agency, perspectives, and experiences, and the underrepresentation of Black narratives of slavery that centralized those aspects. This reality called attention to different ways of thinking about and studying the relationships between the fictive and the historical, the imaginative and the archival, and the false and the true.

Without a doubt, the 1970s witnessed a flourishing in Black women's literary production, and this period, unsurprisingly, has been aptly termed the Black Women's Literary Renaissance. This era also marked the beginning of a renaissance of post–civil rights narratives of slavery, and given Black women's roles in writing a significant number of these texts, it does not surprise that the increase in post–civil rights narratives of slavery overlaps with the Black Women's Literary Renaissance, as Black women writers profoundly shaped the development of this genre. In the decade prior, the 1960s had witnessed what Madhu Dubey has identified as Black Power literature of slavery. But whereas this Black Power literature of slavery, which men mostly wrote, consistent with Black Power discourses more generally, rejected philosophies and approaches the civil rights movement had taken toward Black people securing civil rights, post–civil rights narratives of slavery offer a different perspective.

Both Black Power literatures of slavery and post–civil rights narratives of slavery share the perspective that the psychological liberation of Black people from the legacies of slavery (and Jim Crow) remains a crucial aspect of Black freedom. Post–civil rights narratives of slavery, however, do not reject the civil rights movement's strategies, nor do they promote or espouse those of the Black Power movement. Instead, these texts allow readers to engage with the historical past (slavery) and present (aftermath of the civil rights movement) to consider *both* the psychological and material ways that slavery and its legacies (and/or Jim Crow and its legacies) persist and matter for contemporary subjects. In *Monstrous Intimacies, Making Post-slavery Subjects*, Christina Sharpe explains it is important to uncover "the everyday mundane horrors that aren't acknowledged to be horrors" because "the everyday violences that Black(ened) bodies are made to bear are markers for the exorbitant freedom to be free of the marks of a subjection in which we are all forced to participate." This work of engaging the psychological impacts of slavery is important because, as Sharpe explains, contemporary subjects are all post-slavery subjects, whom slavery affects in known and unknown ways.

8. Author Zora Neale Hurston, whose book *Their Eyes Were Watching God* (1937) became pivotal in the Black Women's Literary Renaissance of the 1970s, attending the New York Times Book Fair in 1937.

Post-civil rights narratives of slavery and interiorities

Equally as important, post-civil rights narratives of slavery also imbue Black characters with complicated and conflicting sets of emotions about slavery and its legacies in order to depict the psychological effects that slavery had on Black people, how Black people navigated and responded to them, and how memories about or from slavery continued to affect the Black characters specifically, and, by extension, Black communities too. On the specific issue of memory, post-civil rights narratives of slavery often consider how Black people who did not experience slavery directly experienced its aftermath, either through shared, collective memories, or because of their material inequalities that had roots in slavery. In Gayl Jones's *Corregidora*, the crux of the protagonist's struggles is figuring out how to navigate the familial burden she carries of keeping her family's memories of slavery alive, without letting the traumas of those memories and experiences foreclose upon her own present and future.

These familial memories, or what Marianne Hirsch refers to as "postmemory," figure significantly in these post-civil rights narratives of slavery as characters grapple with the traumas of ongoing racial disenfranchisement and feel these inherited traumas overshadowing their present-day lives. The task, then, for the protagonist Ursa in *Corregidora* is to mitigate, if not altogether alleviate, a displacement or evacuation of the self. Ursa recognizes the force of this postmemory: "[I]t was as if their memory, the memory of all the Corregidora women, was her memory too, as strong with her as her own private memory." Ursa ultimately learns how to honor the experiences and memories of her foremothers without letting them dominate her own life, memory, or future. Arguably, the post-civil rights narratives of slavery provide strategies for how individuals and society more broadly can achieve these goals. These narratives emphasize Black people's interiority in ways that sometimes eluded the autobiographical narratives of slavery due to the political purposes they often served.

By externalizing Black characters' innermost feelings, thoughts, reflections, and ideas, post–civil rights narratives of slavery emphasize the importance of understanding the psychic and psychological dimensions of slavery as critical to the success of Black freedom struggles. In Toni Morrison's now famous essay "The Site of Memory," Morrison defines Black interiority, explains why autobiographical narratives of slavery possess a less pronounced interiority, and argues that contemporary interiority can elucidate historical interiorities, and vice versa. The last point anchors part of the historical, imaginative, cultural, literary, and affective work that post–civil rights narratives of slavery perform as they explore the peculiar institution and its legacies. Morrison's Pulitzer Prize–winning novel *Beloved* (1987) reveals and unfolds the artistic and political visions that "The Site of Memory" articulates.

When Morrison wrote *Beloved*, for example, she wanted precisely to address the complexities of the Black experience during slavery—the interior life that Black people certainly experienced during slavery but that the autobiographical narratives of slavery often omitted or muted. As Morrison herself put it, "the absence of the interior life, the deliberate excising of it from the records that the slaves themselves told," provided an opportunity for the fictive works to "fill in the gaps," to critically fabulate, to underscore the complex, complicated, and contradictory feelings, emotions, thoughts, and experiences Black people possessed about themselves, their lives, their communities, and the United States. These post–civil rights narratives of slavery more deliberately move toward and focus on the interiority of Black life. They offer that another key to understanding the legacies of slavery is comprehending its psychic and psychological dimensions as Black interiority expresses them.

Interiority in this context emphasizes the deepest, most intimate aspects of the Black experience, the feelings, perspectives, and emotions that often remain, to invoke a phrase from W. E. B. Du Bois, "behind the veil." That is, slavery and Jim Crow create racial dynamics that alienate and diminish the expression of Black interiority such that Black communities shielded that interiority from the white gaze. Though shielded, the interiority is always present and that is a key point that post–civil rights narratives of slavery make. Cinematic narratives of slavery emphasize Black interiority, too, in their representations of different types of narratives of slavery, from the autobiographical ones (*Twelve Years a Slave*) to the post–civil rights ones (*The Underground Railroad*).

The complicated dimensions of sexual violence that the autobiographical narratives of slavery and the post–civil rights narratives represent, for example, helpfully point to the ways that post–civil rights narratives approach historical omissions, delve into intimate psychological interiorities, and aid readers in interpreting the silences and/or omissions in autobiographical narratives of slavery. Take as an example how Harriet Jacobs's *Incidents in the Life of a Slave Girl* shies away from detailing the particularities of the sexual torment Dr. Flint inflicts upon her, leaving readers to wonder exactly what Flint did, whether he in fact raped her, and, if he did not rape her, why he wouldn't have engaged in the perversions of sexuality that slavery made permissible and commonplace. Much of Jacobs's interior life remains unarticulated, despite the intimate details she reveals.

But the historical contexts, social norms, and literary expectations that silence this expression in Jacobs's text fall away in post–civil rights narratives of slavery such as Toni Morrison's *Beloved*, Gayl Jones's *Corregidora*, and Sherley Williams's *Dessa Rose*, where Black women's various forms of sexual exploitation under slavery and their feelings about them emerge explicitly and forcefully. In *Beloved*, for example, the text recalls the protagonist's (Sethe) disgust at having to "pay" with sex to have her daughter's name

(Beloved) engraved on the tombstone, "but those ten minutes she pressed up against dawn-colored stone studded star chips, her knees wide open as the grave, were longer than life, more alive, more pulsating than the baby blood that soaked her fingers like oil." The fact that Sethe experienced ten minutes as "longer than life" reinforces the point that the sexual violence against Black women during slavery was often lasting, brutal, and everywhere. *Beloved* does not leave the sexual violence of slavery to innuendo or speculation. Rather, it positions it as quotidian and routinely intertwined with the racial and gender dynamics that slavery upheld.

The examination of interiority in post–civil rights narratives of slavery also provides a methodology to read and analyze autobiographical narratives of slavery. It encourages readers to consider the ways that interiority manifests itself in autobiographical narratives of slavery to insist that readers—then and now—may have underappreciated the significance of Black interiority in this body of literature. It would be erroneous, for example, to argue that *Incidents in the Life* lacks interiority while *Beloved* possesses it. Instead, the insights *Beloved* provides can help readers to analyze where and how interiority emerges in the autobiographical narratives of slavery—and other texts as well—while acknowledging how historical contexts shape the different ways interiority emerges. Whereas post–civil rights narratives of slavery emphasize interiority as part of the freedom dreaming and freedom obtaining, autobiographical narratives of slavery intimate some degree of interiority even if they mainly focused on immediate physical liberation.

Post–civil rights narratives and memories of the past and present: Gayl Jones's *Corregidora*

Divided into five chapters, and spanning a roughly twenty-year span of the life of the protagonist, Ura, *Corregidora* (1975) examines how familial obligation and individual will conflict, how gender expectations complicate Black people's interpersonal and intimate relationships, how the sexual traumas of slavery haunt Black women who experienced them directly as well as their descendants, how slavery differed across the Black diaspora, the role art can play in recording history and inaugurating social change, how heterosexism and homophobia impede the development of homosocial bonds, how reconciliation can occur in Black heterosexual relationships, and how psychic liberation remains key to personal and political transformations in the post–civil rights era.

In *Corregidora*, Jones uses memories—whether they are familial, interpersonal, individual, or collective—to turn readers' attention to the traumatic imprint that slavery has had on the enslaved *and* their descendants, and to provide strategies on how to navigate slavery's psychic and psychological holds. The narrative follows the life of a blues singer, Ursa Corregidora, whose great-grandmother and grandmother have instructed her to "make generations"—that is, to give birth to (women) children. For the Corregidora women, this command to make generations is important because the offspring serve a specific purpose: they are to keep the memories and experiences of their foremothers alive by bearing witness to a history of enslavement and bodily exploitation that they experienced under slavery, but that the Brazilian government tried to deny by destroying all official written histories of slavery. For Gram, Ursa's grandmother, and Great Gram, Ursa's great-grandmother, "making generations" functions as a way to preserve their familial history, and as a way to hold the Brazilian government accountable for the atrocities it committed.

Ursa's foremothers commit to "make generations" in order to provide "evidence" against the Brazilian government (which had permitted rape) and the individuals (Old Man Corregidora's descendants, for example) when they are able to hold them accountable for the crimes committed. As Great Gram admonishes, "The important thing is making generations. They can burn the papers but they can't burn conscious, Ursa. And that what makes the evidence. And that's what makes the verdict." Reproduction, in this context, becomes another way to rewrite or recast the history of Black enslavement, to prevent it from erasure, and to subvert a site of disempowerment—the womb—by reclaiming it as one of power. It also becomes the primary way through which the women define themselves.

The immediate setting of the text covers the years 1947 through 1969, and this time period also works to call into question the role reproduction will play in Black freedom struggles more generally. That is, on the one hand, *Corregidora* sympathizes with and supports the broader call to expand the archive of sources from which to learn about slavery, to emphasize Black women's and Black people's perspectives and experiences in studying slavery, and to address the psychological impacts slavery had alongside its material ones. On the other, *Corregidora* rejects the idea that Black women's contributions to understanding slavery, its legacies, and future nation-building must necessarily be bound to their reproductive roles.

For instance, Jones contrasts Old Man Corregidora's ability to manipulate Ursa's foremother's bodily autonomy with her husband Mutt's desire to control her body and employment choices. The text emphasizes the similarities across national boundaries and historical eras to show that in the historical and contemporary periods Black women's bodily autonomy remains a key site of struggle—whether in the context of white supremacy and racism or the legacies of slavery and Jim Crow as they interact with Black heteropatriarchy. In many ways, Black Power philosophies that championed Black women's reproductive capabilities as their most useful and valuable contributions to Black freedom struggles hover in the text, and Jones fundamentally rejects them, or at least questions their usefulness.

(After all, to be free includes being free to choose not to "make generations" should a woman so choose.)

Ursa's ambivalence toward having children, and ultimate inability to give birth, compel her to find an alternative way to make generations, which for Ursa is singing the blues. A hysterectomy requires Ursa having to find an alternative if she desires to uphold her foremothers' plan for accountability, but *Corregidora* remains unclear as to whether Ursa slips and falls, or whether Mutt pushes her and she falls when she is attempting to explain why she needs the procedure. This ambiguity emerges in the different language Ursa uses throughout the narrative to describe the incident. In many respects, however, the hysterectomy, while traumatic, ends the dilemma Ursa confronts. During her recovery, Ursa thinks, "I'll sing it as you talked it, your voice humming, sing about the Portuguese who fingered your genitals. His pussy. The Portuguese who bought slaves and paid attention only to the genitals. Slapped you across the cunt till it was bluer than black. Concubine daughter." By noting that she will sing the story of the suffering of the generations before her, but that she'll do so using her foremothers' voice, Ursa sees her singing as an extension of her foremothers' imperative that still allows her to transmit the history even if it is through a different medium. By having Ursa use her art, rather than her body, to tell her family's story, Jones emphasizes the role that cultural production will continue to have in revisiting, revising, recording, and rewriting narratives of slavery in the post–civil rights era.

By allowing Ursa to "make generations" through blues performances, Jones situates Ursa within a genealogy of Black blues performers whose song lyrics have called attention to and challenged white supremacy and domestic violence. Jones also clarifies that the blues allows Ursa to disrupt the traumatic hold that the imperative to make generations has held on Ursa's psyche. Although Ursa does not "get over" the trauma, per se, she does learn how to navigate it so that her own memories and experiences do not become, to quote from Hirsch, "evacuated by those of a previous generation." While her foremothers fundamentally reject Ursa's replacement of biological reproduction with the blues, *Corregidora*'s engagement with the psychic holds of slavery and Jim Crow in the text suggests that Ursa must in fact make a different decision, to disrupt the cycle. This phrase, the *psychic hold of slavery*, refers to the various ways—implicitly or explicitly, conscious or unconscious—that slavery's racial logics and organizing principles continue to shape a contemporary subject's actions or thinking.

The psychic hold of slavery: Managed, but not destroyed

Without a doubt, Ursa experiences the directive to make generations as overwhelming, suffocating, and all-encompassing. It permeates her thoughts and demonstrates how her "postmemory" affects a descendant of slavery. She witnesses the ways that "making generations" consumes her foremothers even when they merely recall their experiences or the directive. Thinking about her relationship with Mutt, for example, she remembers a detail about her mother's failed relationship:

> It was as if my mother's whole body shook with that first birth and memories and she wouldn't make others and she wouldn't give those to me, though she passed the other ones down, the monstrous ones, but she wouldn't give me her own terrible ones. Loneliness. I could feel it, like she was breathing it.... Desire, too.... But now when I look back, that's all I see. Desire, and loneliness. A man left her. Still she carried their evidence, screaming, fury in her eyes, but she wouldn't give me that, not that one.

In this reflection, Ursa realizes that by holding on to the imperative to make generations, her mother, Irene, lets go of the ability to develop an intimate relationship. She has "their evidence" and all the trauma associated with it, and she also has a loneliness that's deep and profound. Ursa understands the "evidence" and "loneliness" as correlative and mutually constitutive.

The psychic hold of the legacy of slavery thus prevents Irene from enacting her own desires and leaves her with loneliness. Ursa realizes that even though Mutt and Old Man Corregidora exhibit similar qualities, they are not in fact the same. This realization for Ursa comes alongside her finding a new way to make generations; her identity and subjectivity are no longer bound to the biological imperative to reproduce. By understanding her subjectivity outside of biological terms, Ursa displaces the very traumatic history and memories that have arrested her for so long. At the end of *Corregidora*, Ursa reconciles with Mutt. Describing this reconciliation, Jones explains that it allows Ursa to "make sense of that history in terms of her own life." Consequently, Ursa "doesn't want to be 'bound' by that history, but she recognizes it as important." For the history not to bind her as tightly as it had, Ursa must first better understand its complexities. With this understanding, Ursa can then rewrite a more nuanced history and develop a new one. Ursa's journey provides a model for attenuating the psychic and psychological holds that slavery has on contemporary subjects.

Representatively, Ursa demonstrates how protagonists in post–civil rights narratives of slavery grapple with clarifying the role that memories from the past have on the present and future. Their negotiation of the traumatic past demonstrates how the literary texts also provided a space for readers to discover models and strategies to respond to the psychological effects that slavery's legacies had on (contemporary) descendants. As do cinematic narratives of slavery, the post–civil rights narratives of slavery insist that the racial hierarchies and disparities that both historical eras enforced continue to matter and affect Black people's opportunities, chances, and outcomes. They also matter to Black people's psyches and the broader national psyche.

Post–civil rights narratives of slavery resist the notion that these psychological and psychic traumas can be overcome and instead suggest they can be better managed. In fact, in some ways, they point to the fact that there are aspects of slavery that remain unknown, and that this unknowability may be part of the psychic element that must be negotiated. On the issue of the unknown, Margo Crawford makes this point in her discussion of what she refers to as post-neo-slave narratives: "If the neo-slave narrative is a revisionist history, the post-neo-slave narrative is a move from the literary imagination that fills in the gaps (what historians cannot know) to the refusal to fill in the gaps but to linger in the unknown." The unknowability of slavery indeed contributes to the psychic dimensions that descendants must engage.

Unlike autobiographical narratives of slavery, post–civil rights narratives of slavery emphasize the psychic and psychological redresses that must underlie any form of reparation for slavery's legacies. This argument carefully avoids using phrases such as "get over slavery or Jim Crow" or "heal from the traumas of slavery or Jim Crow" because the post–civil rights narratives of slavery themselves call into question whether such a goal is achievable or desirable. Put another way, they help readers to reconsider what "getting over" or "healing" entails, just as they question what constitutes "freedom" in the aftermath of slavery and the modern civil rights movement.

Thus, post–civil rights narratives of slavery centralize memories—good, bad, traumatic, and otherwise—as significant events or episodes that protagonists must integrate into their own experiences and perspectives in order to live with them (and not be bound by them). For the protagonists who do not achieve this integration, the traumas of slavery (and Jim Crow) ever haunt them. Because these narratives deal with the conditions of the past as much as they do those of the present, this perspective also suggests that society itself cannot move beyond the strains of slavery and Jim Crow either without reconciling the psychic and psychological harm the peculiar institution inflicted (in addition to the material harm it caused). The intrusion of the historical past into the present (Toni Morrison's *Beloved*) or the transportation from the present to the past (Octavia Butler's *Kindred*) amplifies this point by showing the continuum of time—the past, the present, and the future—as constantly affecting and informing each other. Black writers have turned attention to how Black people have imagined this perspective and highlighted these vantage points in their post–civil rights narratives of slavery that emphasize the importance of the legacies of Jim Crow and slavery.

Chapter 6
Black interiority visualized: Cinematic narratives of slavery

"Y'all taught these pickaninnies to give a proper talk," Cora admires. "There's no pickaninnies here, Cora, just children," Georgina clarifies. This exchange between Cora and Georgina occurs at a crucial moment in episode 8 of Amazon Prime's *The Underground Railroad* (2021), a cinematic adaptation of Colson Whitehead's post–civil rights narrative of slavery, the novel *The Underground Railroad* (2016). Cora, who has self-emancipated, but whom the law defines as a fugitive, finds herself trying to adjust to freedom on the Valentine farm in Indiana. Georgina, one of the townspeople, instructs Cora that she must shake the psychological shackles of slavery, and throughout, Royal, another community member in whom Cora confides, continues to emphasize this necessity for Cora. But in this early conversation in the episode, Cora reveals that, despite now residing in an all-Black community, she unknowingly and subconsciously retains some of racial logics of slavery, as her description of the children as "pickaninnies" reveals.

Georgina accentuates slavery's lasting influence when, after Cora apologizes for the pickaninny faux pas, she reassures Cora that "often times when folks' minds finally get free, they have to unlearn as much as they learned." Instructively, Georgina foreshadows the ways that memories of slavery will continue to infringe upon Cora ("finally get free") and impact her ability to

9. In a scene from *The Underground Railroad*, Georgina (Kara Flowers, left) and Cora (Thuso Mbedu, right) walk through the community and discuss the importance of freeing one's mind from slavery. This conversation occurs immediately after the children recite parts of the Declaration of Independence, which leads Cora to remark that the "pickaninnies" had given a good speech.

experience a freedom that is more than a release from physical bondage. Through this conversation between Cora and Georgina, *The Underground Railroad* suggests that memories of slavery will continue to haunt the formerly enslaved unless they "unlearn" the racial logics that helped to maintain the peculiar institution. By using the verb "unlearn," Georgina emphasizes the *active* role that the formerly enslaved must take in also becoming free from slavery's psychic and psychological hold. The *Underground Railroad* series underscores this point by juxtaposing Cora's current thoughts, feelings, interactions, and experiences with flashbacks to slavery.

The absence of quotidian instances of white supremacy in Georgina's self-sufficient Black community dulls their sense of any immediate potential violence from their surrounding white neighbors. As far as they are concerned, prior to Cora's arrival, the community lives in a prosperous safe haven, free from the encroachments of white supremacy and anti-Black racism. They thus believe Cora's presence increases the possibility for a confrontation and threatens their sense of security; the Fugitive Slave Act of 1850 makes Cora's physical freedom precarious, as it legally facilitates her potential re-enslavement. That some townspeople do not want her to remain for this very reason heightens her awareness of her *outsider* status and her continued attachment to slavery. On the very day that the townspeople meet to debate whether they should expel Cora, the white neighbors incite a massacre and effectually destroy the town and Black community. Although the massacre occurs during a meeting where the community members wrangle over whether Cora should remain, the episode clarifies that Cora's presence does not in fact cause the massacre. Rather, the white neighbors admit that because members of the all-Black community had viewed themselves and their community as equal to white people and theirs, they had to destroy it. Indeed, the Black people's talent, success, and ambition incited white rage.

Although Cora survives and flees, the episode parallels the community's experience as "free" with Cora's as "self-emancipated" to show how white supremacy and anti-Black racism threatened all forms of Black life and living. The precariousness of Cora's status emerges clearly: she is physically free but can be readily apprehended, and slavery's logics weigh heavily on her thinking and memories. But the town's freedom, as the massacre shows, is tenuous, too, albeit in a different way. By underestimating how the racial logics of slavery persist around them, the Valentine community miscalculates the always present threat of white supremacy; while they have prepared for potential violence, they do not realize all of those who could be the source of it; that is, they do not think of their immediate neighbors as potential threats. These juxtapositions between Cora and the community members, between outsider and the insider statuses, between Black prosperity and white rage, and between remembering and forgetting, reveal the complex ways that slavery's psychological and psychic elements impact the formerly enslaved and the enslaved. In many ways, Cora's quest for physical freedom coincides with her journey for psychological liberation, and *The Underground Railroad*, like many other cinematic narratives of slavery, parallels these experiences to emphasize the importance of both physical and psychological freedoms from the implicit and explicit attachments to the racial logics of slavery.

Cinematic narratives of slavery: Black-centered perspectives and interiorities

American chattel slavery has occupied the Black artistic imagination during the early decades of the twenty-first century. Since 2000, Black cultural producers have used cinematic narratives of slavery to respond to contemporary calls for racial justice that have demanded a better understanding of how slavery and its legacies continue to shape American society. Through these narratives of slavery, (Black) cultural producers have desired to represent slavery from Black(er) perspectives, examine how slavery still impacts contemporary social and political relationships, imagine an interior Black life during slavery, show how Black people created community and developed intimate relationships despite slavery's dehumanizing conditions, and fill in or correct historical gaps about slavery. In some ways, cinematic narratives of slavery complement and represent noncinematic post–civil rights narratives of slavery, and autobiographical narratives of slavery in particular. They also extend narratives of slavery to audiences who primarily consume knowledge through visual media. The adaptation of written texts to cinematic ones further evidences this claim. From movies to television series, from the mainstream Hollywood theaters to independent ones, from DVDs to digital platforms such as Amazon Prime, cinematic narratives of slavery have found a diverse set of venues and audiences to share their creative works.

Some of these cinematic narratives of slavery include *The Underground Railroad* (Amazon Prime, 2021), *The Underground* (CW, then Hulu, 2016), *Twelve Years a Slave* (2013), *The Book of Negroes* (2015), *Django Unchained* (2012), *The Birth of a Nation* (2016), *Emancipation* (2022), and *Kindred* (Hulu, 2022). Twenty-first-century cinematic narratives of slavery do in fact build upon cinematic representations of slavery that emerged in earlier eras, but they include more Black people and perspectives at different stages of the production process, even if they, similar to their predecessors, are not completely produced by Black people. When non-Black people are involved in these twenty-first-century narratives, however, they maintain the goal of decidedly centering Black perspectives in ways that Julia Dash's *Sankofa* (1993), Steven Spielberg's *Amistad* (1997), and Jonathan Demme's *Beloved* (1998), which is an adaptation of Toni Morrison's post–civil rights novel (1987), for example, did in the 1990s, as they more forcefully represented Black perspectives. The 1990s works, in many ways, diverge from their 1970s predecessors, when films such as *Drum* (1976) and *Mandingo* (1975) emerged as popular yet problematic representations of slavery. Not only did those films reinforce white supremacy by not centering Black voices and perspectives and relying upon racial stereotype and caricature, but they also emphasized the need for white saviors.

Mainstream narratives of slavery in the twenty-first century still do not interrogate white supremacy, even as they move away from explicitly anti-Black iconography. Monica Ndounou argues that the tendency to promote racial reconciliation without interrogating systemic racism or white complicity in slavery undermines the potential of these narratives to undo the harms that slavery has inflicted materially and psychologically. This phenomenon creates the need for "revolutionary films about slavery [that] tend to focus on Black experiences of slavery, to foreground Black agency in liberation struggles, and to reject the white savior formula and racial reconciliation narrative." Films that are not revolutionary "tend to be harmful to Black people as misrepresentation affects social relations." Films that better represent the complexities of slavery can potentially improve social relations materially and psychologically *and* not put forth additional harm.

As an instructive example of twenty-first-century cinematic narratives of slavery, we can look to Nate Parker's *The Birth of a Nation*, which demonstrates a host of issues that Black narratives of slavery take up. Like other works of its genre, it explores slavery and its legacies and works to sharpen citizens' understanding of the interiority and intimate details of Black life during (and after) slavery. By examining the intricate ways that the protagonist's work as itinerant preacher, familial relationships, and a sense of racial community influence his decision to liberate the enslaved Black people in his community, we can see how and why Black cinematic narratives of slavery aim to show the brutality of slavery as an institution, the cruelty of enslavers, the psychological grip that slavery holds on the enslaved and possibly their descendants, the various forms of resistance the enslaved enacted, the ways that the enslaved formed community and family, the epistemologies about race and white supremacy that the enslaved shared, and the sustained efforts the enslaved took to live beyond slavery's limitations (sometimes even understanding the limitations that would exist after Emancipation).

Birth of a Nation, or death of a nation: Parker on Griffith

D. W. Griffith's *Birth of a Nation* (1915) is one of the most (in) famous (master) cinematic narratives of slavery that emerged in the early twentieth century. It worked diligently to reinforce white supremacy and to reassert the image of Black inferiority and savagery that had consistently breathed life into slavery. In Nate

Parker's *The Birth of a Nation* (2015), Parker invokes the title of Griffith's film to turn the ideologies it promotes on their head and offer a perspective of how enslaved Black people resisted the savagery of white supremacy and enslavement through armed resistance. The contrast between Parker's and Griffith's representations in many ways underscores the stakes of Black perspectives foregrounding Black experiences when discussing slavery and its enduring legacies. As Parker explains in an interview with Kam Williams:

> [I]t isn't often, as Black men, that we get an opportunity in Hollywood to play a leading role with a strong character. . . . plus the narrative isn't usually controlled by us. So I asked myself, if I could tell any story, which would it be? And Nat Turner being my hero from a social justice standpoint, he became the focus of my desires when it came to making a film. I just wanted to create a hero that added to the narrative of America who didn't look like the usual patriots.

By retelling and reframing the story of Nat Turner as a hero, as a patriot, Parker points to his desire to challenge mainstream narratives and redefine what it means to be a patriot, to live up to the ideals of freedom and democracy in the midst of enslavement. This shift in perspective and the redefining of *patriotism* illuminate a broader trend in which Black artists, activists, politicians, and ordinary citizens use terms and symbols that emblematize "democracy" or "democratic principles" to call for civil rights and citizenship rights for Black people.

Griffith's representation of race relations essentially argued that the absence of slavery had placed society in disarray during and after Reconstruction. Slavery's violence—the actual violence and threat of potential violence—no longer served as effective tools to control Black men's supposed unbridled sexuality. As a result, Black men had been able to run wild, upending society in general, and threatening the purity of white women's sexuality in particular. The film called upon familiar and popular stereotypes about Black people and avoided emphasizing how white supremacy's systematic denial of Black people's rights to full citizenship after slavery ended had thrown society into disarray. Griffith's film emblematized the types of cultural representations that Ida B. Wells's Jim Crow narrative of slavery, *A Red Record*, had anticipated and rejected.

While the buck/brute stereotype purportedly evidenced the need to forcibly control Black men, in the post-Emancipation era it circulated to confirm the failure of Reconstruction to effectively socialize and humanize the alleged eternal beast. In one of the 1915 film's most discussed scenes, Gus, played by a white man in Blackface, chases Flora, a white woman, who ultimately falls to her death rather than have a Black man touch her, let alone potentially rape her. The film's perspective remained clear: the country had erred in ending slavery and Reconstruction had disrupted the order slavery had provided by allowing Black men into social and political spaces for which they were ill-equipped to handle the responsibilities. The message it sent emerged more clearly: even if the United States could not return to slavery in name, white supremacy could extend slavery's mechanisms of control. The violence the film generated, the extension of Jim Crow segregation throughout society, and additional ideological and material assaults on Black life that emerged suggest that viewers understood what the film intended to convey.

Films such as *Birth of a Nation* lamented the bygone era of slavery *and* called for the institution of an analogous form of social, political, and economic control. For Black viewers and critics, white supremacy persists throughout *Birth of a Nation*, but viewers downplay its persistence because there is a broader American obsession with Black savagery that Griffith taps into. When Gus chases Flora, for example, the scene purposefully appears to invite violence against Black people by playing into a stereotype that had resonated for decades across the South; its political impact emerged in lynching justifications, anti-miscegenation laws, and Black Codes more generally. In other words, by positing that Black people's behaviors justify the violence against them, the film reinforces the ideas that the post-Emancipation challenges Black people endured resulted from their behaviors and/or own inaction. As ubiquitous as white supremacy and anti-Black racism remain in the film—and society more generally—neither they, nor their relationship to slavery, get treated as the root causes of continued Black disenfranchisement after Emancipation.

Cinematic narratives of slavery: Visually righting the past

In many ways, Parker's *The Birth of a Nation* provides a useful entry point to think more representatively about the ways that Black cinematic narratives of slavery in the twenty-first century examine both the present and the past to appreciate slavery's continued influences and Black people's continued engagements. The film takes the historical Nat Turner as its point of departure and focuses on what historians have described as one of the most important and violent *rebellions* that the enslaved undertook. But *The Birth of a Nation* does not cast the events as either a rebellion, insurrection, or uprising as dominant historical narratives have. Instead, it positions the events as God-inspired acts of self-emancipation that resulted from the *immorality* of slavery, including the laws, customs, and policies that allowed the system to function. Self-emancipation, as a concept, rejects the historical weight of terms such as "uprising" that criminalized these acts of resistance and that suggested the existing laws against which the self-emancipators fought were actually just (even if legal). In other words, the film not only nods toward the ways that the Second Great Awakening shaped the religious-political consciousness of enslaved Black people, abolitionists, and pro-slavery advocates, but, pointedly, it also suggests that the nation truly cannot be born, or come to life, until slavery is abolished. Parker visually depicts the violence that David Walker warns against in his *Appeal.*

Parker carefully outlines the destructiveness of white supremacy to nation-building by keeping the violence of white supremacy—in its quotidian, interpersonal, structural, ideological, and material ways—on full display throughout the film. Parker emphasizes violence as characteristic of and endemic to white supremacy. This perspective indeed acknowledges Griffith's portrayal, which treats white supremacy, anti-Black racism, and white control of Black life and Black sexuality as the pillars of nation-building and national thriving. But Parker's film refuses to cast white supremacy's violence as an ordinary and reasonable "reaction" to Black intrusion or entrance into white life as Griffith had done. Parker explains:

> I deliberately want[ed] to tether the present to 1915 in order to create a context as to why we are where we are. Griffith, in my opinion, may have been one of the most powerful people around in the sense that he inspired all of America to embrace white supremacy as a form of self-preservation. As a son of the Confederacy, he asked America to turn its back on any solidarity with people of color with the hopes that whites would be able to maintain their privilege forever.

Parker argues that white supremacy, anti-Black racism, and white dominance do not have to undergird nation-building. His film attempts to reject the normalization of these ideas and practices that Griffith, mirroring the nation, had championed.

Yet it is equally as important to accentuate Parker's insistence that Black people's own epistemologies, acts of resistance, and bodily autonomy remain central to the nation's ability to function as a democracy. Parker thus guides the viewer to several interior episodes of Black life, with the intent of showing more depth into the Black psyche. Viewers embark upon a journey into Black people's social customs, religious practices, intimate relationships, interpersonal interactions, spheres of influence, disagreements and arguments, and everyday experiences that happen in the crucible of enslavement. This focus on an interior Black life, even in enslavement, is a distinctive aim that twenty-first-century Black cinematic narratives of slavery desire to achieve.

Cinematic narratives of slavery: Nat Turner and the cinematic imagination

The Birth of a Nation follows the journey of the protagonist, Nat Turner, whose religious experiences, literacy, oratory skills, and relationship with his owner increase his exposure to slavery's cruelties. These experiences also heighten his awareness of the role Christianity can play in emancipating the enslaved, and they allow him to influence the purchase of an enslaved woman who eventually becomes his wife. Collectively, these experiences solidify his resolve to emancipate himself and other enslaved Black people. Driving the plot are white owners sharing an economic interest in securing and maintaining the racial hierarchy that slavery provides, as well as the financial gains they accrue from it. Nat's reputation as a gifted preacher precedes him, and other plantation owners become aware of his status as a "Nigger" preacher. One of the townspeople who knows that Nat's owner continues to experience financial difficulties offers the owner an opportunity that will enrich them both. Their plan is seemingly simple: they will travel to other plantations, allow Nat to preach, and reap the financial compensation that Nat's preaching creates.

All of Nat's invitations to preach, of course, carry strict instructions; in particular, Nat must encourage the enslaved to remain obedient to their owners. The owners solicited Nat's services to send *one* and *one message only*—that the enslaved must obey their masters. The owners believe the prospect of "unrest" is emerging and therefore want Nat to quell any potential dissent. But the fears of unrest are rooted in any action the enslaved take up, including expressing the desire to eat more than one meal per day. Undoubtedly, this plan to include Nat hinges on his race as a Black man and his status as an enslaved person. The plan and its racial dynamics crystallize: have Nat, an enslaved Black man, confide in his racial peers that God has ordained Black people to remain subservient and beholden to the will of their owners. As one owner puts it when he introduces Nat, "Got a preacher here tonight . . . and he's a nigger like y'all. And he's here to talk to you about the Lord. Now listen to him and you just might make it into heaven." For this owner, freedom for enslaved Black people can only be otherworldly, and even that possibility hinges on earthly submission.

By having a Black preacher reinforce the logics of white supremacy, the owners believe they are effectively tricking the enslaved to believe they rightfully belong enslaved. While the threat of violence and actual violence that slavery provides do not need Nat to convey this message in order for the owners to maintain their power, having Nat convey it can help. But, as the scenes in the film clarify, Nat's sermons repulse the enslaved more than they compel submission. This disconnect between the owners' intent and the effect the sermons have on the enslaved ultimately leads to Nat rejecting the plan. In other words, Nat's status as a "nigger like y'all" does more to undermine the institution of slavery than it does to support it.

Nat's racial identification with the enslaved, belief in a higher moral authority, and witnessing of quotidian and extreme forms of violence against the enslaved on other plantations undo his early willingness to comply. Even when Nat initially acquiesces to the plan and preaches submission, he remains visibly uneasy. Tears linger in his eyes, his voice trembles, and he falters and stammers to articulate the message. After the owner on their first stop implores him to preach, and watches and listens carefully, Nat opens his bible and shares: "Brothers and sisters, I lead you, I lead you to, Peter 2:18. 'Slaves submit yourselves to your masters with all respect. Not only to those who are good and considerate but also to those who are harsh.'" His physical *presentation* during this scene, and during the entirety of his itinerant preaching journey, starkly contrasts with the affect and demeanor he possesses when preaching to his home community; the film juxtaposes his latter despair with his former joy to evidence the conflict this traveling assignment presents for Nat. The desperation he sees in the listeners' eyes only sharpens his inner conflict; they stare and they scowl, but refuse to applaud or say "amen" as a sign of their affirmation, agreement, or acceptance.

The final scene that Nat preaches rejects messages of submission, and, in a debate with one of the white men, he elaborates on his understanding of Christianity that leads him to forcefully preach liberation instead. In a verbal battle royale, Nat eviscerates biblical justifications for slavery and Black inferiority. For each assertion of Black submission that the white man justifies with a scriptural reference, Nat offers an alternative scripture to rebut it. The two men are actively debating and yelling at each other until Nat's owner intercedes to reprimand Nat for "talking to" a white man in this way. The scene ends with Sam (Nat's owner) admonishing him, "don't you eyeball me boy," and then knocking his teeth out with the barrel of a gun. He then instructs a bystander to "get him to the post." Notably, Nat's position within the community deteriorates when he openly contests ideas about Black people's alleged inferiority, a position that his own status in the community undermines. In the scene that follows, Nat receives what viewers are led to believe is his first beating. If it is not his first one, it certainly is his most brutal. His owner punctuates his return from the whipping post by asking and demanding, "Have you learned your lesson, boy?!" Nat has indeed learned a lesson, but not the one his owner desires. Instead, Nat learns that freedom must be pursued, vigorously, and at whatever costs.

Earlier freedom dreams lay the foundation

This moment culminates in Nat's decision to emancipate himself and others, yet *The Birth of a Nation* parallels a range of incidents that also raise in Nat and his followers the desire to secure their own freedom. The film treats two of Nat's childhood experiences within his Black community as critical to his development and then stages two adulthood ones as equally as formative. As the film opens, viewers see the Black community participating in a naming ceremony that invokes the names of African ancestors and that demonstrates the importance of cultural traditions, family, and community despite what slavery prohibits. Shortly following, Nat returns from playing only to find that the older children have eaten the meager supply of food before he can get his portion. His father, Isaac, decides to procure food for them, but white patrollers stop him. Defending himself, he kills one of them, grabs Nat and the food, and flees back to their cabin.

When the white men arrive to apprehend Isaac, they question Nat's grandmother, mother, and even Nat himself, who understands the ways of slavery; following the lead of the adults, he, too, insists he has not seen his father, despite having been in the woods with (and slightly ahead of) his father when the patrollers pursue. In an important deathly yet comical moment, one of the cans of food they had secured begins to roll toward one of the white men's feet; quickly, Nat's grandmother drops to the floor, conceals the rolling can, and implores, "Massa, please." Thwarting the white men's ability to see the food, Nat's grandmother removes the present danger and saves their lives. In these moments, Nat witnesses Black ingenuity, resourcefulness, creativity, family, and community. The film ties these moments together as significant building blocks that shape Nat's early consciousness about race and justice.

Critics have expressed concern about *The Birth of a Nation*'s development—or lack thereof—of Black women characters, yet concerns for Black women's bodily autonomy, protecting them from rape in particular, also further Nat's resolve to emancipate himself and his community. Heteropatriarchal ideas about gender may guide Nat's motives, but this fact does not negate how the ambition to protect Black women from the sexual violence of slavery resonates. Rape and the always imminent possibility of rape remain part and parcel of the daily lives of enslaved Black women—a point that Harriet Jacobs's *Incidents in the Life of a Slave Girl* goes to great lengths to emphasize. *The Birth of a Nation* shows Cherry, Nat's wife, landing in the cross-hairs of licentious white men as she tried to obtain water. That a quotidian and trivial task can easily result in rape emphasizes the pervasiveness of sexual violence under slavery. Although the film does not show the rape itself, the aftermath of Cherry's recovery clarifies what indeed had happened. Cherry survives the rape yet apologizes for its occurrence.

Nat rejects the idea that Cherry's behavior invited the rape when he admonishes her against apologizing, and the film furthers this point by having the episode occur while she attempts to complete a mundane daily chore. Not only does Nat advise her that "you don't owe that to nobody," but he also vows "I'ma take care of it." Cherry, however, cautions Nat against avenging her violation, and reminds him that Jesus said, "Put up again thy sword into its place: for all they that take the sword shall perish with the sword." Rather than deterring Nat, Cherry's prescient warning in fact compels Nat to reconsider his own role—as an instrument of God—in facilitating the liberation of the enslaved. If Cherry's rape raises this consideration for Nat, Esther's rape exerts full pressure on his need to accept his role as a liberator. Nat cannot persuade his owner Sam to deny a request that makes Esther available for rape. Discouraged by his inability to protect Esther from rape, Esther's husband demands, "Where is He, Nat? Where is God now?" Together, these scenes of sexual violation reveal how the desire for Black women's bodily autonomy also shapes Nat's consciousness and his ultimate decision to liberate his community.

When he does so, he informs the enslaved Black community that "your earthly master is gone. You are free. Our ancestors and unborn children rejoice." By connecting the enslaved to both the ancestors and the unborn, Nat's freedom mission avenges the past, corrects the present, and, importantly, paves the way for full citizenship rights for future generations.

By convincing his comrades that they should begin to liberate the enslaved Black community, Nat insists that Black people's own efforts will be necessary to destroy slavery and white supremacy. Nat and his army enact a spree of killings that the film does not shy away from to demonstrate how, in their estimation, they must kill white people and white supremacy simultaneously. The violence of white supremacy must be met with armed resistance, they believe. Pointedly, Sam and his white friend who raped Esther become the first two to die, with Nat and Esther's husband, respectively, killing them. Particularly noteworthy in this final portion are the reflections that the Black soldiers offer to explain why they have chosen to fight. They recognize they may not survive, and they know that some of the other Black men have perished already. Yet they renew their commitment to freedom by rejecting how slavery had controlled their time and movement. For instance, as they prepare to battle, Nat asks what time it is, and notes that it is approximately 5:30 a.m. At this juncture, the men reflect on what they *normally* would be doing. Nat shares, "By now I'd be two rows down, bout half a bag full," referring to his responsibilities of picking cotton. Another notes, "I'd be headed to the barn, getting ready to feed the stock." And a final one relays, "I'd be boiling water in the smokehouse, thinking about dumping it on Massa's head," to great laughter.

Collectively, the soldiers' comments express a vision for life that exceeds the limits slavery had placed upon them, and underscore why they are willing to die while fighting for their freedom. That they laugh at the prospect of one man contemplating "dumping it on Massa's head" provides insights into the interior thinking and

10. In a scene from *The Birth of a Nation*, Nat Turner (Nate Parker) leads the remaining Black soldiers as they prepare for what will be their final battle, and they discuss what they normally would be doing at 5:30 a.m. as sunbreaks and the day begins. The battle that follows ultimately concludes the liberation journey that the men had undertaken and that Nat Turner has led.

feelings that these Black men possessed. They fight *and* they play, they work *and* they laugh, they experience hurt *and* they experience love. By foregrounding these Black perspectives and interiorities, *The Birth of a Nation* shows, despite the undoubtedly and indisputably harsh conditions of slavery and battle, that Black people had time for quotidian thoughts and experiences. This scene recalls earlier ones where Black people laugh, marry, and celebrate insofar as it emphasizes a Black experience and life that extends beyond the abjection/destituteness that slavery intended to place on Black life.

The Birth of a Nation concludes with Nat's army failing to complete its ambitious task of abolishing slavery. White men capture Nat and then publicly hang him as a warning—a precursor to post-Emancipation lynching—against trying to challenge the status quo of enslavement. But the film points to these actions as being critical to future Black freedom struggles. As the film concludes, information about the historical Nat Turner flashes across the screen alongside the laws that local governments enacted in an effort to curtail future resistance movements from enslaved Black people following the historical event. This ending functions to restore the historical Nat Turner as a Black freedom fighter. He is not, for example, a deranged Black man suffering from hallucinations that God inspired him. This portrayal of the interiority of Turner and his community members shows how enslaved Black people pulled all levers to which they had access to abolish slavery *and* create meaningful relationships, communities, and psychological bonds.

Cinematic narratives of slavery: Challenges and opportunities for viewers

For viewers, cinematic narratives of slavery can be challenging to watch. The violence of slavery that they depict—or that viewers imagine they will show—can result in viewers preferring to avoid them. Why, after all, would someone pay to witness a traumatic history that may seem disconnected from the contemporary moment? Cinematic narratives of slavery nonetheless often take as fact the idea that the legacies of slavery matter in the present. By better understanding this traumatic yet pivotal era in American history, citizens who watch these films or series can become better equipped to respond to contemporary sociopolitical realities. This is a point, for example, that Steve McQueen emphasizes when he discusses his motivations for directing *Twelve Years a Slave* (2013), a cinematic adaptation of Solomon Northup's as-told-to autobiographical narrative of slavery, *Twelve Years a Slave, Narrative of Solomon Northup, a Citizen of New-York, Kid-napped in Washington City in 1841, and Rescued in 1853.*

Cinematic narratives of slavery therefore ask viewers to connect the past to the present, to consider how knowledge about the relationship between historical eras can shape the future, and to manage the emotional responses that these representations may generate. There is no way to produce a cinematic narrative of slavery without representing—without actually showing on screen—the material and ideological violence that slavery and white supremacy inflicted upon Black people. But, as do contemporary narratives of slavery that place Black perspectives as the foci, these cinematic narratives of slavery really emphasize the many steps Black people took to resist the economic, physical, and spiritual exploitations that slavery readily attempted. The balance between these forces—white supremacy, Black resistance, and Black community formation—has kept critics, producers, supporters, and viewers actively questioning the degree to which and what types of violence remain integral to how the narratives unfold.

Richard Iton addresses this concern, noting that the visual may "impede attempts to transmit more nuanced and substantive sentiments because the crowding out effect of the visual and the tendency of the camera to seek out spectacular and merely shocking, perhaps exciting rather than provocative and paradigm shifting ones." Gratuitous or excessive violence can interrupt the ability of cinematic narratives of slavery to (re)shape public opinion about slavery and its legacies. Rather than engaging more, viewers who witness excessive violence might become overwhelmed and instead disengage. In Saidiya Hartman's examinations of slavery's violence, she similarly wonders how to "give expression to these outrages without exacerbating the indifference to suffering that is the consequence of the benumbing." Rather than display the "shocking and the terrible," she instead looks "elsewhere and consider[s] those scenes in which terror can hardly be discerned." Other critics too have looked toward the quotidian—the ordinary places where violence and its threats loom—to show the horrifying aspect of slavery's brutality and to turn some attention away from the spectacular abuse of Black bodies vis-à-vis voyeuristic spectatorship.

Given the pervasiveness of violence, its quotidian manifestations, and the ubiquity of the denial or diminishment of both of these truths, cinematic narratives of slavery find themselves in a quandary as they navigate this particular issue. In many ways, for example, the cinematic narratives of slavery try to help viewers to visualize the violence that nineteenth-century autobiographical narratives of slavery forcefully stated (Douglass's characterization of beatings), or that they allude to but do not detail explicitly (Jacobs's recollection of sexual harassment). They also try to portray the psychological interiority that the autobiographical narratives sometimes imply and that post–civil rights narratives of slavery imagine and represent more explicitly (Morrison's *Beloved*).

But how many such scenes do viewers need to see—or care to see—in order to understand slavery better or remind them of white supremacy's indifferent brutality? How many scarred backs; hanged, but not killed, Black bodies; sexually harassed and/or forcibly raped Black women; mothers crying as owners nonchalantly sell their children; Black people jumping into the Atlantic Ocean to self-emancipate; Black people getting thrown into the Atlantic Ocean; or scenes of a general anti-Black racism that disdains Black people and Black life?

These questions, as important as they are, cannot overshadow the main point that cinematic narratives of slavery that focalize Black experiences make about the violence of slavery: the violence was brutal, and always a threat. Yet violence did not become the sine qua non of Black experience during enslavement. To emphasize this point, cinematic narratives of slavery displace the violence from the center of Black life to instead consider the ways Black people created lives and communities in spite of these circumstances.

Therefore, cinematic narratives of slavery, by focusing on and emphasizing Black feelings, experiences, epistemologies, and thinking, shift viewers' attention to important aspects of Black sociality. By making these aspects their focus, such twenty-first-century Black narratives of slavery reshape viewers' understanding of Black sociality and Black interiority. They represent Black people creating and recognizing extended kin networks; debating paths forward for Black political, civic, and economic empowerment; discussing the persistence of white supremacy and its embeddedness in society and the law; demonstrating love and tenderness toward each other; embracing and recognizing marriages; expressing emotional vulnerability in interpersonal relationships; arguing and disagreeing with each other; and desiring sex and engaging in sexual activities.

By turning attention to the complexity of Black life during slavery, cinematic narratives of slavery assume Black people's humanity and their related abilities to reason and feel. They are in fact people, people who happen to be enslaved but certainly not simply or only "slaves." They stress the aspects of life—relationships, rituals, feelings—that would endure in Black communities beyond Emancipation and into the present day, just as they did before slavery. Parker observes that "I use that film designed to disenfranchise and terrorize us as a starting point with the hope that, by reclaiming and re-purposing it, we could right a massive wrong since we're still dealing with the fallout of the terror that it inspired." Righting the wrong not only requires the shift toward Black perspectives in cinematic narratives of slavery; it also requires, as Parker suggests by insisting that "we're still dealing with the fallout," understanding the specific ways that past injustices—the legacies of slavery—still matter in the contemporary period in order to address the legacies of slavery and Jim Crow that persist and matter still.

Epilogue: The longest afterlives ever: Legacies of slavery and Jim Crow

Slavery and its legacies are both everywhere and nowhere at the same time. On the one hand, citizens acknowledge that slavery and its legacies have had an indelible imprint on the United States' history, culture, politics, wealth, education, healthcare, and so forth. In other words, for those of us who study slavery, for those who live in the afterlives of slavery (and Jim Crow), and for those allies who listen, read, and otherwise pay attention, the argument is simply put like this: there is not an institution in the United States that currently exists that slavery (and its legacies) did not build, shape, or, at the very least, impact.

On the other hand, or perhaps on the same one, resistance to this claim persists and emerges from a wide range of people. Objectors cannot, or, perhaps more accurately, they refuse to, fathom the possibility that more than 300 years of slavery and 100 years of legalized Jim Crow segregation might have produced the inequalities that persist in American society, and that, in some ways, these inequalities have grown more intractable since the passing of civil rights legislation in the mid-1960s. But a quick lesson in math might challenge this thinking. For example, it is indisputable that 400 (the years of persistent, legalized discrimination against Black people that set them at all types of disadvantages) is greater than 60 (the number of years that have passed since civil rights legislation allowed Black people to access institutions that had previously excluded them). The idea that 60 years would undo the cumulative effect of 400 plus years of systemic, systematized, and seismic racial inequities seems implausible. Yet this claim undergirds some of the explanations for racial inequities and disparities that underestimate—if not altogether deny—the significance of the legacies of slavery and Jim Crow. Of course, anti-Black racism and white supremacy remain co-contributors and co-conspirators to these explanations. And, of course, the denial of anti-Black racism and white supremacy as explanatory reasons keeps both forces invisible and empowered. This point underscores the importance of making them visible, identifying how they work, explaining the effects of their work, and proposing solutions to mitigate and possibly undo the harms they have done and continue to do.

Objectors, for example, attribute racial inequalities to white people earning their wealth through hard work and a fair system of meritocracy that rewards them for it. If Black people worked harder, changed their behaviors, they too could share wealth. Neither slavery, sharecropping, separate and *inherently unequal* accommodations and facilities, redlining, anti–affirmative action rulings, nor predatory lending has had an enduring impact from their vantage points. While perhaps unfortunate aspects of American history and experience, the ideas and policies that maintained these practices no longer exist—so this perspective maintains. With their elimination, Black people have equal access, and therefore their outcomes, or lack thereof, result from their effort, or lack thereof—so the thinking goes. While perhaps appealing, this explanation falls short of appreciating the enduring effects of discrimination. The reasoning, too, at its best is sophistry. At its worst, it is racist and anti-Black. This racist anti-Black sophistry has risen to new heights in the federal government's attempt to criminalize, mischaracterize, and roll back diversity, equity, and inclusion initiatives in 2025. The willingness of institutions, corporations, and individuals to capitulate makes the work of this volume and artists even more urgent.

In other words, while prevalent and popular, arguments that deny the legacies of slavery and Jim Crow, and that explain inequalities as the result of Black people's lack of effort or initiative, are historically myopic, purposefully ignorant of cause and effect, and willfully accepting of racial injustices. As long as these perspectives prevail, the need and urgency for Black narratives of slavery will persist. Black cultural producers will continue to complicate these arguments, reject their premises, show the interconnection between the past and present, and provide solutions for how to lessen the effects of these inequities and achieve some parity. Historically, the exclusion of Black people from formal political activities such as voting intensified their use of art to make the case for Black people's rights. In the contemporary period, the purposeful erosion of Black people's political, cultural, civil, educational, and economic rights will keep this trend alive. But beyond this point, Black artists have a clear sense of the roles that representation plays in creating and dispersing knowledge and how Black cultural production has moved, and can continue to move, the needle on understanding how slavery and its legacies must be understood better and more fully.

Even if the US Congress will not pass legislation to institute an official "Commission to Study and Develop Reparation Proposals for African Americans" to study slavery, to determine its long-term effects and legacies, and to propose remedies to alleviate those effects, such as reparations, Black cultural producers have been engaged in this work for what seems like the longest time ever. All the while, they, too, start with an assumption that unfortunately still needs to be stated: Black people are people who possess the range of emotions, experiences, contradictions, insights, and flaws characteristic of humans more broadly. And that Black lives and perspectives do in fact matter and are necessary to understand the legacies of slavery and its subsequent experiences in Jim Crow. If such a commission were to pass Congress and a president were to sign it into law, Congress's first source of study should be Black narratives of slavery to understand the complexity of the problem and gain insights on solutions. Black archives, like Black lives, matter, especially since Black people have been the ones thinking about, writing about, and living with the longest afterlives ever: the legacies of slavery and Jim Crow!

References

Chapter 1: Black narratives of slavery and Black cultural production

Jennifer Morgan, *Reckoning with Slavery: Gender, Kinship, and Capitalism in the Early Black Atlantic* (Duke University Press, 2001), 64.

Saidiya Hartman, "Venus in Two Acts," *Small Axe* 26 (2008): 1–14.

Rinaldo Walcott, *The Long Emancipation: Moving toward Black Freedom* (Duke University Press, 2001), 4.

David Walker, *Walker's Appeal in Four Articles: Together with a Preamble, to the Coloured Citizens of the World, but in Particular, and Very Expressly, to Those of the United States of America* (Forgotten Books, 2017), 18, 19.

Martin Delany, *The Condition, Elevation, Emigration, and Destiny of the Colored People of the United States* (A Public Domain Book, 2012), 2.

Chapter 2: Autobiographical narratives of slavery

Frederick Douglass, *Narrative of the Life of Frederick Douglass, an American Slave, Written by Himself* (Modern Library, 2004), 7, 44, 60.

Harriet Jacobs, *Incidents in the Life of a Slave Girl, Written by Herself* (Modern Library, 2004), 119, 121, 216, 151, 180.

Shateema Threadcraft, *Intimate Justice: The Black Female Body and the Body Politic* (Oxford University Press, 2016), 38.

Chapter 3: Not written by themselves: Oral yet recorded narratives of slavery

Sharon Musher, "The Other Slave Narratives: The Works Progress Administration Interviews," in *The Oxford Handbook of the African American Slave Narrative*, ed. John Ernest (New York: Oxford University Press, 2016), 106.

Federal Writers' Project, *Alabama WPA Slave Narratives: From Interviews with Former Slaves* (Historic Publishing, 2017), 20.

Federal Writers' Project, *Virginia Slave Narratives: Slave Narratives from the Federal Writers' Project, 1936–1938* (Applewood Books, 2006), 2.

William Still, *The Underground Railroad Records: Narrating the Hardships, Hairbreadth Escapes, and Death Struggles of Slaves in Their Efforts for Freedom* (Random House, 2019), 341.

Chapter 4: Slavery remade: Jim Crow narratives of slavery

Gene Jarrett, *Representing the Race: A New Political History of African American Literature* (New York University Press, 2011), 9.

Kevin Gaines, *Uplifting the Race: Black Leadership, Politics, and Culture in the Twentieth Century* (University of North Carolina Press, 2012), 21.

Carol Anderson, *White Rage: The Unspoken Truth of Our Racial Divide* (Bloomsbury, 2017), 3.

Booker T. Washington, *Up from Slavery: An Autobiography* (Modern Library, 1999), 101, 145–146.

Jarvis Givens, "Introduction," in *Booker T. Washington: Up from Slavery* (Norton Library, 2023), vi–xxvi.

Ida B. Wells, *Crusade for Justice: The Autobiography of Ida B. Wells* (University of Chicago Press, 2000), 53, 57.

Ida B. Wells, *A Red Record: Tabulated Statistics and Alleged Cause of Lynching in the United States* (Compass Circle, 2019), 6.

Koritha Mitchell, *From Slave Cabins to the White House: Homemade Citizenship in African American Culture* (University of Illinois Press, 2019), 2.

Chapter 5: Freedoms on their minds: Post-civil rights narratives of slavery

Angelyn Mitchell, *The Freedom to Remember: Narrative, Slavery, and Gender in Contemporary Black Women's Fiction* (Rutgers University Press, 2002), 4.

Madhu Dubey, "Freedom Now: Black Power and the Literature of Slavery," in *Black Cultural Production after Civil Rights*, edited by Robert J. Patterson (University of Illinois Press, 2019), 30.

Christina Sharpe, *Monstruous Intimacies: Making Post-slavery Subjects* (Duke University Press, 2010), 3–4.

Marianne Hirsch, "The Generation of Postmemory," *Poetics Today* 29, no. 1 (2008), 107.

Toni Morrison, *Beloved* (Penguin Books, 1988), 5.

Toni Morrison, "The Site of Memory," in *What Moves at the Margin* (University Press of Mississippi, 2008), 65–80.

Gayl Jones, *Corregidora* (Beacon Press, 1987), 22, 52, 101.

Gayl Jones, "Interview with Gayl Jones," *Callaloo* 16, no. 2 (1982), 45.

Margo Crawford, "The Inside-Turned-Out: Architecture of the Post-Neo-Slave Narrative," in *The Psychic Hold of Slavery: Legacies in American Expressive Culture* (Rutgers University Press, 2016), 71.

Chapter 6: Black interiority visualized: Cinematic narratives of slavery

Barry Jenkins, dir., *The Underground Railroad* (Amazon Prime Video, 2021).

Monica White Ndounou, "Slavery Now: 1970s Influence Post-20th-Century Films on American Slavery," in *Black Cultural Production after Civil Rights*, ed. Robert J. Patterson (University of Illinois Press, 2019), 76.

Nate Parker, "Nate Parker: The 'Birth of a Nation' Interview," African American Literature Book Club, October 4, 2016, https://aalbc.com/interviews/interview.php?id=1829.

Nate Parker, dir., *The Birth of a Nation* (Fox Searchlight, 2016).

Richard Iton, *In Search of the Black Fantastic: Politics and Popular Culture in the Post-Civil Rights Era* (Oxford University Press, 2008), 106.

Saidiya Hartman, *Scenes of Subjection: Terror, Slavery, and Self-Making in Nineteenth Century America* (Oxford University Press, 1999), 4.

Further reading

Abdur-Rahman, Aliyah. *Against the Closet: Black Political Longing and the Erotics of Race*. Duke University Press, 2012.

Andrews, William. *Slavery and Class in the American South: A Generation of Slave Narrative Testimony, 1845–1860*. University of North Carolina Press, 2019.

Andrews, William. *To Tell a Free Story: The First Century of Afro-American Autobiography, 1760–1865*. University of Illinois Press, 1988.

Brown, Kimberly. *The Repeating Body: Slavery's Visual Resonance in the Contemporary*. Duke University Press, 2015.

Byer, Keith. *Remembering the Past in Contemporary African American Literature*. University of North Carolina Press, 2005.

Colbert, Soyica, Aida-Levy-Hussen, and Robert Patterson, eds. *The Psychic Hold of Slavery: Legacies in American Expressive Culture*. Rutgers University Press, 2016.

Commander, Michelle, ed. *Unsung: Unheralded Narratives of American Slavery and Abolition*. Penguin Classics, 2021.

Davis, Thulani. *The Emancipation Circuit: Black Activism Forging a Culture of Freedom*. Duke University Press, 2022.

Dubey, Madhu. *Black Women Novelists and the Nationalist Aesthetic*. Indiana University Press, 1994.

Dubey, Madhu. "Speculative Fictions of Slavery." *American Literature* 82, no. 4 (2010), 779–805.

Eaves, Shannon. *Sexual Violence and American Slavery: The Making of Rape Culture in the Antebellum South*. University of North Carolina Press, 2024.

Ernest, John. *The Oxford Handbook of the African American Slave Narrative*. Oxford University Press, 2014.
Eyerman, Ron. *Cultural Trauma: Slavery and the Formation of African American Identity*. Cambridge University Press, 2002.
Freeburg, Christopher. *Counterlife: Slavery after Resistance and Social Death*. Duke University Press, 2021.
Goyal, Yogita. *Runway Genres: The Global Afterlives of Slavery*. New York University Press, 2019.
Hine, Darlene Clark. "A Black Studies Manifesto." *The Black Scholar: Journal of Black Studies and Research* 44, no. 2 (2014), 11–15.
Hutchins, Zachary. *Before Equiano: A Pre-history of the North American Slave Narrative*. University of North Carolina Press, 2022.
Jones, Nikole-Hannah, ed. *The 1619 Project: A New Origin Story*. One World Press, 2021.
Keizer, Arlene. *Black Subjects: Identity Formation in the Contemporary Narrative of Slavery*. Cornell University Press, 2004.
Keizer, Arlene. "Obsidian Mine: The Psychic Aftermath of Slavery." *American Literary History*. 24, no. 4 (2012), 686–701.
Levy-Hussen, Aida. *How to Read African American Literature: Post-Civil Rights Fiction and the Task of Interpretation*. New York University Press, 2016.
Marable, Manning. *Race, Reform, and Rebellion: The Second Reconstruction and Beyond in Black America, 1945–2006*. University of Mississippi Press, 2017.
McBride, Dwight. *Impossible Witnesses: Truth, Abolition, and Slave Testimony*. New York University Press, 2001.
McDowell, Deborah. "In the First Place: Making Frederick Douglass and the Afro-American Narrative Tradition." In *African American Autobiography: A Collection of Critical Essays*, edited by William Andrews. Prentice Hall, 1993, 36–58.
McDowell, Deborah, and Arnold Rampersad, eds. *Slavery and the Literary Imagination*. John Hopkins University Press, 1989.
McHenry, Elizabeth. *To Make Negro Literature: Writing, Literary Practice, and African American Authorship*. Duke University, Press, 2021.
Milteer, Warren Eugene, Jr. *Beyond Slavery's Shadow: Free People of Color in the South*. University of North Carolina Press, 2021.
Moore, Kelli. *Legal Spectatorship: Slavery and the Visual Culture of Domestic Violence*. Duke University Press, 2022.

Neary, Janet. *Fugitive Testimony: On the Visual Logic of Slave Narratives*. Fordham University Press, 2017.

Nunley, Tamika. *At The Threshold of Liberty: Women, Slavery, and Shifting Identities in Washington, D.C.* University of North Carolina Press, 2021.

Painter, Nell Irvin. *Sojourner Truth: A Life, a Symbol*. W. W. Norton, 1997.

Rushdy, Ashraf. *Neo-Slave Narratives: Studies in the Social Logic of a Literary Form*. Oxford University Press, 1999.

Stauffer, John. "Abolition and Slavery." In *The Oxford Handbook of Slavery in the Americas*, edited by Robert L. Paquette and Mark M. Smith. Oxford University Press, 2010.

Stepto, Robert. "Distrust of the Reader in Afro-American Narratives." In *Reconstructing American Literary History*, edited by Sacvan Bercovitch. Harvard University Press, 1986.

Tillet, Salimishah. *Sites of Slavery: Citizenship and Racial Democracy in the Post–Civil Rights Imagination*. Duke University Press, 2016.

Washington, Margaret. *Sojourner Truth's America*. University of Illinois Press, 2009.

Woolfork, Lisa. *Embodying American Slavery in Contemporary Culture*. University of Illinois Press, 2011.

Wong, Edlie. *Neither Fugitive nor Free: Atlantic Slavery, Freedom Suits, and the Legal Culture of Travel*. New York University Press, 2009.

Index

Note: Figures are indicated by an italic '*f*', respectively, following the page number.

For the benefit of digital users, indexed terms that span two pages (e.g., 52–53) may, on occasion, appear on only one of those pages.

A

B

C

D

E

F

G

H

I

J

K

L

M

N

O

P

R

S

T

U

V

W

AFRICAN HISTORY

A Very Short Introduction

John Parker & Richard Rathbone

Essential reading for anyone interested in the African continent and the diversity of human history, this *Very Short Introduction* looks at Africa's past and reflects on the changing ways it has been imagined and represented. Key themes in current thinking about Africa's history are illustrated with a range of fascinating historical examples, drawn from over 5 millennia across this vast continent.

> 'A very well informed and sharply stated historiography . . . should be in every historiography student's kitbag. A tour de force . . . it made me think a great deal.'
>
> Terence Ranger,
> **The Bulletin of the School of Oriental and African Studies**

www.oup.com/vsi

Human Rights

A Very Short Introduction

Andrew Clapham

An appeal to human rights in the face of injustice can be a heartfelt and morally justified demand for some, while for others it remains merely an empty slogan. Taking an international perspective and focusing on highly topical issues such as torture, arbitrary detention, privacy, health and discrimination, this *Very Short Introduction* will help readers to understand for themselves the controversies and complexities behind this vitally relevant issue. Looking at the philosophical justification for rights, the historical origins of human rights and how they are formed in law, Andrew Clapham explains what our human rights actually are, what they might be, and where the human rights movement is heading.

www.oup.com/vsi

LINCOLN

A Very Short Introduction

Allen C. Guelzo

The award-winning Lincoln authority Allen C. Guelzo offers here a penetrating look into the mind of one of our greatest presidents. The author takes us on a wide-ranging exploration of seven problems that confronted Lincoln, setting these problems and Lincoln's responses against the larger world of trans-Atlantic liberal democracy in the 19th century, comparing Lincoln not just to Andrew Jackson or John Calhoun, but to British thinkers such as Cobden, Bentham, and Bright, and to French observers de Tocqueville and Guizot.

www.oup.com/vsi

RACISM

A Very Short Introduction

Ali Rattansi

From subtle discrimination in everyday life and scandals in politics, to incidents like lynchings in the American South, cultural imperialism, and 'ethnic cleansing', racism exists in many different forms, in almost every facet of society. But what actually is race? How has racism come to be so firmly established? Why do so few people actually admit to being racist? How are race, ethnicity, and xenophobia related? This book reincorporates the latest research to demystify the subject of racism and explore its history, science, and culture. It sheds light not only on how racism has evolved since its earliest beginnings, but will also explore the numerous embodiments of racism, highlighting the paradox of its survival, despite the scientific discrediting of the notion of 'race' with the latest advances in genetics.

www.oup.com/vsi

BIOGRAPHY

A Very Short Introduction

Hermione Lee

Biography is one of the most popular, best-selling, and widely-read of literary genres. But why do certain people and historical events arouse so much interest? How can biographies be compared with history and works of fiction? Does a biography need to be true? Is it acceptable to omit or conceal things? Does the biographer need to personally know the subject? Must a biographer be subjective? In this *Very Short Introduction* Hermione Lee considers the cultural and historical background of different types of biographies, looking at the factors that affect biographers and whether there are different strategies, ethics, and principles required for writing about one person compared to another. She also considers contemporary biographical publications and considers what kind of 'lives' are the most popular and in demand.

> 'It would be hard to think of anyone better to provide a crisp contribution to OUP's Very Short Introductions.'
>
> **Kathryn Hughes, The Guardian**

www.oup.com/vsi